Chinese

IN MINNESOTA

Sherri Gebert Fuller

Foreword by Bill Holm

MINNESOTA HISTORICAL SOCIETY PRESS

Publication of this book was supported, in part, with funds provided by the June D. Holmquist Publication Endowment Fund of the Minnesota Historical Society.

www.mnhs.org/mhspress

The Minnesota Historical Society Press is a member of the Association of American University Presses.

Manufactured in Canada

10 9 8 7 6 5 4 3 2 1

International Standard Book Number: 0-87351-470-X

♾ The paper used in this publication meets the minimum requirements of the American National Standard for Information Sciences Permanence for Printed Library Materials, ANSI Z 39.48-1984.

Library of Congress Cataloging-in-Publication Data

Fuller, Sherri Gebert.
   Chinese in Minnesota / Sherri Gebert Fuller ; foreword by Bill Holm.
      p.   cm. — (The people of Minnesota)
   Includes bibliographical references (p.) and index.
   ISBN 0-87351-470-X (pbk. : alk. paper)
      1. Chinese Americans—Minnesota—History. 2. Chinese Americans—Minnesota—Social conditions. 3. Minnesota—History. 4. Minnesota—Ethnic relations. I. Title. II. Series.

F615.C5F85   2004
977.6'004951—dc22
                                                             2003017205

This book was designed and set in type by Wendy Holdman, Stanton Publication Services, St. Paul, Minnesota; it was printed by Friesens, Altona, Manitoba.

Contents

Foreword
by Bill Holm

Human beings have not been clever students at learning any lessons from their three or four thousand odd years of recorded history. We repeat our mistakes from generation to generation with tedious regularity. But we ought to have learned at least one simple truth: that there is no word, no idea that is not a double-edged sword. Take, for example, the adjective *ethnic*. In one direction, it cuts upward, to show us the faces, the lives, the histories of our neighbors and ourselves. It shows us that we are not alone on this planet—that we are all rooted with deep tendrils growing down to our ancestors and the stories of how they came to be not *there*, but *here*. These tendrils are visible in our noses and cheekbones, our middle-aged diseases and discomforts, our food, our religious habits, our celebrations, our manner of grieving, our very names. The fact that here in Minnesota, at any rate, we mostly live together in civil harmony— showing sometimes affectionate curiosity, sometimes puzzled irritation but seldom murderous violence—speaks well for our progress as a community of neighbors, even as members of a civilized human tribe.

But early in this new century in America we have seen the dark blade of the ethnic sword made visible, and it has cut us to the quick. From at least one angle, our national wounds from terrorist attacks are an example of ethnicity gone mad, tribal loyalty whipped to fanatical hysteria, until it turns human beings into monstrous machines of mass murder. Few tribes own a guiltless history in this regard.

The 20th century did not see much progress toward solving the problem of ethnicity. Think of Turk and Armenian, German and Jew, Hutu and Tutsi, Protestant and Catholic, Albanian and Serb, French and Algerian—think of our own lynchings. We all hoped for better from the 21st century but may not get any reprieve at all from the tidal waves of violence and hatred.

As global capitalism breaks down the borders between nation-states, fanatical ethnicity rises to life like a hydra. Cheerful advertisements assure us that we are all a family—wearing the same pants, drinking the same pop, singing and going on line together as we spend. When we invoke *family*, we don't seem to remember well the ancient Greek family tragedies. We need to make not a family but a civil community of neighbors, who may neither spend nor look alike but share a desire for truthful history—an alert curiosity about the stories and the lives of our neighbors and a respect both for difference—and for privacy. We must get the metaphors right; we are neither brothers nor sisters here in Minnesota, nor even cousins. We are neighbors, all us *ethnics*, and that fact imposes on us a stricter obligation than blood and, to the degree to which we live up to it, makes us civilized.

As both Minnesotans and Americans, none of us can escape the fact that we *ethnics*, in historic terms, have hardly settled here for the length of a sneeze. Most of us have barely had time to lose the language of our ancestors or to produce protein-stuffed children half a foot taller than ourselves. What does a mere century or a little better amount to in history? Even the oldest settlers—the almost ur-inhabitants, the Dakota and Ojibwa—emigrated here from elsewhere on the continent. The Jeffers Petroglyphs in southwest Minnesota are probably the oldest evidence we have of any human habitation. They are still and will most likely remain only shadowy tellers of any historic truth about us. Who made this language? History is silent. The only clear facts scholars agree on about these mysterious pictures carved in hard red Sioux quartzite is that they were the work of neither of the current native tribes and can be scientifically dated only between the melting of the last glacier and the arrival of the first European settlers in the territory. They seem very old to the eye. It is good for us, I think, that our history begins not with certainty, but with mystery, cause for wonder rather than warfare.

In 1978, before the first edition of this ethnic survey appeared, a researcher came to Minneota to interview local people for information about the Icelanders. Tiny though their numbers, the Icelanders were a real ethnic group with their own language, history, and habits of mind. They settled in the late 19th century in three small clumps around Minneota. At that time, I could still introduce this researcher to a few old ladies born in Iceland and to a dozen children of immigrants who grew up with English as a second language, thus with thick accents. The old still prayed the Lord's Prayer in Icelandic, to them the language of Jesus himself, and a handful of people could still read the ancient poems and sagas in the leather-covered editions brought as treasures from the old country. But two decades have wiped out that primary source. The first generation is gone, only a few alert and alive in the second, and the third speaks only English—real Americans in hardly a century. What driblets of Icelandic blood remain are mixed with a little of this, a little of that. The old thorny names, so difficult to pronounce, have been respelled, then corrected for sound.

Is this the end of ethnicity? The complete meltdown into history evaporated into global marketing anonymity? I say no. On a late October day, a letter arrives from a housewife in Nevis, Minnesota. She's never met me, but she's been to Iceland now and met unknown cousins she found on an Internet genealogy search. The didactic voice in my books reminds her of her father's voice: "He could've said that. Are we *all* literary?" We've never met, she confesses, but she gives me enough of her family tree to convince me that we might be cousins fifteen generations back. She is descended, she says with pride, from the Icelandic law speaker in 1063, Gunnar the Wise. She knows now that she is not alone in history. She has shadowing names, even dates, in her very cells. She says—with more smug pride—that her vinarterta (an Icelandic immigrant prune cake that is often the last surviving ghost of the old country) is better than any she ate in Iceland. She invites me to sample a piece if I ever get to Nevis. Who says there is no profit and joy in ethnicity? That killjoy has obviously never tasted vinarterta!

I think what is happening in this letter, both psychologically and culturally, happens simultaneously in the lives of hundreds of thousands of Minnesotans and countless millions of Americans. Only the details differ, pilaf, jiaozi, fry bread, collards, latkes, or menudo rather than vinarterta, but the process and the object remain the same. We came to this cold flat place so far from the sea in wave after wave of immigration—filling up the steadily fewer empty places in this vast midsection of a continent—but for all of us, whatever the reason for our arrival: poverty, political upheaval, ambition—we check most of our history, and thus our inner life, at the door of the new world. For a while, old habits and even the language carry on, but by the third generation, history is lost. Yet America's history, much less Minnesota's, is so tiny, so new, so uncertain, so much composed of broken connections—and now of vapid media marketing—that we feel a loneliness for a history that stretches back further into the life of the planet. We want more cousins so that, in the best sense, we can be better neighbors. We can acquire interior weight that will keep us rooted in our new homes. That is why we need to read these essays on the ethnic history of Minnesota. We need to meet those neighbors and listen to new stories.

We need also the concrete underpinning of facts that they provide to give real body to our tribal myths if those myths are not to drift off into nostalgic vapor. Svenskarnas Dag and Santa Lucia Day will not tell us much about the old Sweden that disgorged so many of its poor to Minnesota. At the height of the Vietnam War, an old schoolmate of mine steeled his courage to confess to his stern Swedish father that he was thinking both of conscientious objection and, if that didn't work, escape to Canada. He expected patriotic disdain, even contempt. Instead the upright old man wept and cried, "So soon again!" He had left Sweden early in the century to avoid the compulsory military draft but told that history to none of his children. The history of our arrival here does not lose its nobility by being filled with draft-dodging, tubercular lungs, head lice, poverty, failure. It gains humanity. We are all members of a very big club—and not an exclusive one.

I grew up in western Minnesota surrounded by accents: Icelandic, Norwegian, Swedish, Belgian, Dutch, German, Polish, French Canadian, Irish, even a Yankee or two, a French Jewish doctor, and a Japanese chicken sexer in Dr. Kerr's chicken hatchery. As a boy, I thought that a fair-sized family of nations. Some of those tribes have declined almost to extinction, and new immigrants have come to replace them: Mexican, Somali, Hmong, and Balkan. Relations are sometimes awkward as the old ethnicities bump their aging dispositions against the new, forgetting that their own grandparents spoke English strangely, dressed in odd clothes, and ate foods that astonished and sometimes repulsed their neighbors. History does not cease moving at the exact moment we begin to occupy it comfortably.

I've taught many Laotian students in my freshman English classes at Southwest State University in Marshall. I always assign papers on family history. For many children of the fourth generation, the real stories have evaporated, but for the Hmong, they are very much alive—escape followed by gunfire, swimming the Mekong, a childhood in Thai refugee camps. One student brought a piece of his mother's intricate embroidery to class and translated its symbolic storytelling language for his classmates. Those native-born children of farmers will now be haunted for life by the dark water of the Mekong. Ethnic history is alive and surprisingly well in Minnesota.

Meanwhile the passion for connection—thus a craving for a deeper history—has blossomed grandly in my generation and the new one in front of it. A Canadian professional genealogist at work at an immigrant genealogical center at Hofsos in north Iceland assures me, as fact, that genealogy has surpassed, in raw numbers, both stamp and coin collecting as a hobby. What will it next overtake? Baseball cards? Rock and roll 45 rpms? It's a sport with a future, and these essays on ethnic history are part of the evidence of its success.

I've even bought a little house in Hofsos, thirty miles south of the Arctic Circle where in the endless summer light I watch loads of immigrant descendants from Canada and the United States arrive clutching old brown-tone photos, yellowed letters in languages they don't read, the misspelled name of Grandpa's farm. They feed their information into computers and comb through heavy books, hoping to find the history lost when their ancestors simplified their names at Ellis Island or in Quebec. To be ethnic, somehow, is to be human. Neither can we escape it, nor should we want to. You cannot interest yourself in the lives of your neighbors if you don't take sufficient interest in your own.

Minnesotans often jokingly describe their ethnic backgrounds as "mongrel"—a little of this, a little of that, who knows what? But what a gift to be a mongrel! So many ethnicities and so little time in life to track them down! You will have to read many of these essays to find out who was up to what, when. We should also note that every one of us on this planet is a mongrel, thank God. The mongrel is the strongest and longest lived of dogs—and of humans, too. Only the dead are pure—and then, only in memory, never in fact. Mongrels do not kill each other to maintain the pure ideology of the tribe. They just go on mating, acquiring a richer ethnic history with every passing generation. So I commend this series to you. Let me introduce you to your neighbors. May you find pleasure and wisdom in their company.

Chinese

IN MINNESOTA

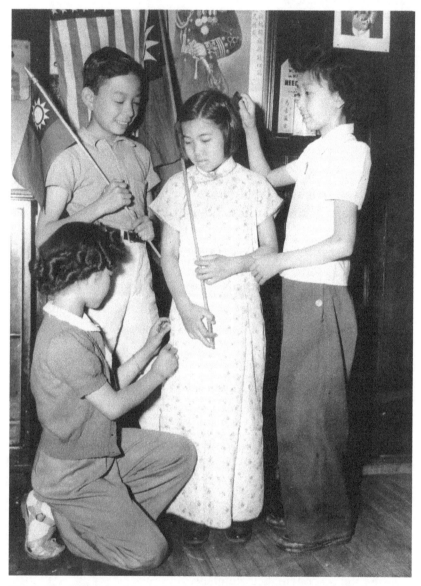

Preparing for a parade or special event, Oy Huie, in traditional Chinese dress and holding a Chinese Nationalist flag, is flanked by James Hong, left, and two unidentified friends, about 1939.

THE LAND OF 10,000 LAKES is seldom, if ever, associated with anything Chinese. Few people realize that the history of the Chinese community dates as far back as those groups typically considered Minnesota's pioneers. While immigrants of European descent long ago found their place in the history books, Chinese immigrants have only slowly been recognized for their struggles and tenacity in the face of harsh immigration laws and job discrimination that persisted well into the 20th century. Influencing and shaping Minnesota history since the early 1870s, Chinese in Minnesota by 2000 numbered 18,622 people and were a vital force in professional, cultural, and educational spheres throughout the state.[1]

Early Immigration

The first significant Chinese immigration to the United States took place after the discovery of gold in California (known as *Gam Saan,* literally Gold Mountain) in 1848. The promise of riches resulted in more than 300,000 Chinese crossing the Pacific from 1850 to 1882 to seek economic betterment. When the panic of 1873 brought economic depression and unemployment to the western states, the Chinese became scapegoats for the American work force who feared their competition in the labor market. Mobs attacked Chinese settlements, lynched immigrant laborers, and burned their houses. In the decades that followed, the anti-Chinese movement spread from the West Coast over the entire nation. Thousands of Chinese left the Pacific states, where the hostility was most severe, some returning to Hawaii or China and others migrating to the Midwest and the East Coast. By 1890 Chinese lived in every state and territory of the United States.

Chinese immigrating to the continental United States

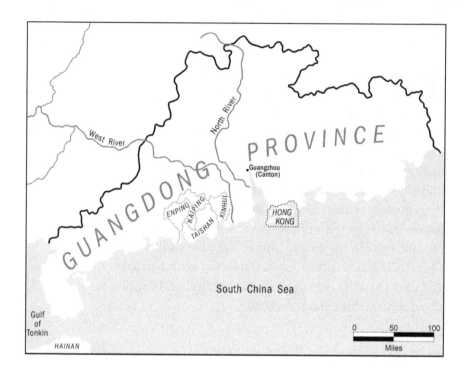

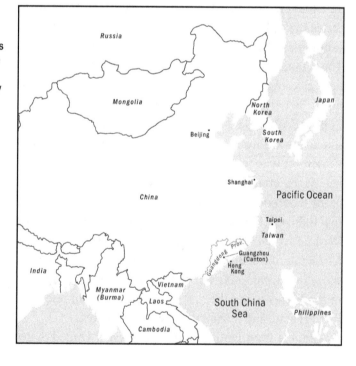

Until the mid-20th century, most Chinese immigrants to Minnesota came from Guangdong Province. Later they arrived from Hong Kong, Taiwan, and northern China as well as from Guangdong.

were predominantly from an area known as *Sze Yup* (Four Districts), which included Enping, Kaiping, Xinhui, and Xinning, later called Taishan (Toishan). A significant percentage of Chinese immigrants in the United States emigrated from Toishan, a rocky, hilly area of small farms that produced only enough food for about a third of its population even in relatively stable times.

Because of the great importance attached to preserving family and ancestral bonds in Chinese traditional culture, families in *Sze Yup* usually chose one male member to emigrate. This individual was expected to send money on a regular basis to support relatives remaining in China. Ideally he married before emigrating, and his wife stayed behind to attend to family members, including his aging parents, and care for the ancestral home and family graves. Many of the early emigrants believed they would return to China to live after a few years of work abroad, but gradual adaptation to the new environment, wars, and hard times often made this difficult, if not impossible.

The first Chinese arrived in Minnesota in the mid-1870s and by 1885 approximately 100 immigrants, all male, were working in Chinese-owned laundries or restaurants. Chinese businesses, including hotels, also appeared in iron range towns during this period, when rapid development of the mining industry caused an unprecedented population boom and a demand for the services Chinese provided.

Meeting the challenge of restrictive job opportunities and discrimination, the creation of laundries and restaurants presented the only employment options available to Chinese. These businesses required little capital investment and, more importantly, did not compete with white labor. Often based on partnerships of brothers or individuals from the same village in China, these early businesses depended for their economic survival on unpaid family help and the low-paid work of new arrivals.[2]

Newspapers from Winona to Sauk Centre announced

A. H. Wing's Chinese Laundry in Winona, about 1881. According to the August 18, 1876, edition of the *Trempeleau Republican*, "A Chinese laundry is to be opened in Winona next week by A. Wing who has lately arrived from Sioux City."

the arrival of the newest immigrants. Reporters' descriptions were brief but mildly inquisitive because the dress, language, and eating habits of the newcomers differed greatly from their own. As noted in the October 11, 1879, issue of the *St. Paul Daily Globe*, residents of Lake City were visiting the "new 'almond-eyed' laundry in large numbers, the great curiosity being the manner in which 'John' partakes of his dish of rice, employing his favorite 'chop sticks' instead of knife, fork or spoon." Once established, the new "laundrymen," as they were often referred to, took advantage of the marketing tools available to them. These entrepreneurs advertised their services in local newspapers, promising that "family and fancy washing could be returned in two days" or created their own business cards for distribution as Sam Lee of Stillwater did in 1879.[3]

The arrival of Chinese immigrants was probably the first time state residents encountered anyone of non-European descent (besides the Ojibwe and Dakota.) What little information was known about Chinese was likely gleaned from publications such as *Northwest Magazine.* An article in the November 1885 issue, entitled "The Chinese Problem," found that "the objection to them is not that they are dirty or drunken. It is that we cannot possibly assimilate them with our American national stock. . . . He subsists on rice and dried fish, with a bit of pork added on Sundays. Even bread, our staff of life, is a luxury to him. He needs no home, for he has no family. Twenty Chinamen will live in a shanty which would not accommodate the family of the poorest Irish laborer."

Quong Long, the operator of a Chinese laundry in Red Wing, about 1883

To offset established stereotypes, lecturers from China such as Foo Chin Wong traveled the United States to speak to interested audiences about the history of their homeland. In January 1877, Wong lectured in Minneapolis, St. Paul, and Owatonna. The January 15, 1877, *Owatonna Journal* noted that "the large immigration of Chinese to this country, of late years, makes any information in regard to that strange and ancient people of peculiar interest to Americans at the present time."

Local Chinese residents also worked hard to challenge

Woo Yee Sing stood in front of Yee Sing Laundry at 1319 Nicollet Ave. in Minneapolis, about 1895. He arrived in Minneapolis about 1880 and became well known for his colorful horse-drawn delivery wagon in the Lowry Hill neighborhood. In addition to his laundry service, he also sold imported tea and chinaware.

unfair viewpoints that saturated mainstream publications. One such individual was Woo Yee Sing, a respected leader of the early Chinese community in Minneapolis. Within the first three years of his arrival in 1880, Woo established a laundry, an import shop, and the Canton Café, thought to be the first Chinese restaurant in Minnesota, on 1st Avenue South. Members of the Westminster Presbyterian Church, active in missionary work in China, invited Woo to attend English classes at their church in 1882. Little did they know what an important anchor the church would become for Chinese immigrants as a point of contact with the larger society.[4]

Shortly after the arrival of Chinese in Minnesota, the United States Congress passed the 1882 Chinese Exclusion Act, the first federal law to bar immigration on the basis of race and class. In 1880 the Chinese represented only .002% of the United States population. This law prohibited skilled and unskilled Chinese laborers from entering the United States for ten years and prevented naturalization of all Chinese immigrants residing in the United States. This law was not only an obstacle to upholding family ties but severely restricted the Chinese community's ability to be accepted into mainstream America. According to historian Erika Lee, the Exclusion Act "helped to define and reinforce understandings of Chinese as 'Orientals' and foreign 'others' who endangered the American nation." Repercussions of

DECORATING CHINA.

This 1882 cartoon from *Harper's Weekly* illustrates the blatant hostility Chinese encountered that eventually led to the passage of the Exclusion Act in 1882. Unfortunately, the act condoned the ongoing mistreatment of Chinese living in the United States.

this act would affect Chinese immigrants and American-born Chinese for years to come.[5]

Nationally the Chinese population declined following enactment of the Exclusion Act, dropping from a high of 107,488 in 1890 to a low of 61,639 in 1920. However, the Chinese population in Minnesota grew steadily from 1876

Legislation Affecting Chinese Americans

1868   The 14th Amendment of the U.S. Constitution stated that a person born in the United States was a U.S. citizen by birth, but the rights of natural born citizenship did not extend to the Chinese until the 1898 U.S. Supreme Court case of *U.S. v. Wong Kim Ark.*

1872   California adopted an anti-miscegenation law that prohibited interracial marriages. It was not until 1967 that the U.S. Supreme Court ruled all anti-miscegenation laws in the nation to be unconstitutional.

1882   The United States passed the Chinese Exclusion Act.

1888   The Scott Act prohibited re-entry of Chinese laborers who had left for China temporarily and wanted to return to America; 20,000 Chinese laborers were denied re-entry when their re-entry permits were invalidated.

1892   The Geary Act extended the Chinese Exclusion Act for another ten years. Chinese aliens had to register with the U.S. government for issuance of a certificate of identity. Police and immigration officials could arrest and deport those without the certificate.

1898   U.S. Supreme Court ruled in the Wong Kim Ark case that native-born Chinese Americans were entitled to constitutional protection and that their citizenship rights cannot be violated.

1904   The Chinese Exclusion Act was extended indefinitely.

1910   The Angel Island Immigration Station in San Francisco Bay was established to process Chinese immigrants; it lasted for three decades.

1922   The Cable Act stripped U.S. citizenship from any woman married to an alien ineligible to citizenship.

1924   The Immigration Act of 1924 (Asian Exclusion Act) banned entry of all aliens ineligible to citizenship.

1927   U.S. Supreme Court ruled that U.S. citizenship rights extended to foreign-born children of an American citizen but not to foreign-born grandchildren whose parents had never resided in the United States.

1943   December 17: the Chinese Exclusion Acts were repealed. The act allowed naturalization for the Chinese in America and established an annual immigration quota of 105 Chinese.

1947   The amended War Brides Act allowed alien wives of Chinese American veterans to immigrate to the United States on a non-quota basis.

1952   The McCarran-Walter Act allowed U.S. naturalization regardless of race, but Asians were still limited with immigration quotas.

1965   The United States passed the 1965 Immigration Act that abolished the national origins quota system that was put into effect by the 1924 Immigration Act.

to 1910, largely through migration from the western states. Certified merchants and their families—exempt from the act—continued to arrive throughout this period. Their financial status and familiarization with American ways often allowed them to escape pervasive discrimination on the West Coast. Laborers, on the other hand, were forced to decide whether they should return to China or remain in this country to work and possibly never see their families again.[6]

When the Exclusion Act was renewed in 1892 as the Geary Act, it called for the creation of Chinese inspectors to monitor movement of Chinese immigrants both nationally and internationally. The federal government established offices at seven ports of entry and metropolitan areas, one of them being Minneapolis. The provisions of the Geary Act required Chinese to register and secure a certificate of residency as proof of their right to be in the United States. Without this paperwork, they faced imprisonment or deportation. Early activities of the state's Chinese inspectors are evident in reports of arrests and deportations of Chinese throughout Minnesota, including Rochester, St. Paul, and Cloquet. An October 31, 1899, article in the *Minneapolis Journal* noted that the deportation of the "Celestials Costs us $500."[7]

Immigration Offices were also responsible for tracking the number of Chinese residing in the state. A May 19, 1905, *Minneapolis Journal* article entitled "Counted the Chinks" stated that the Immigration Office conducted a census and determined that 261 Chinese were living in Minnesota: 86 in Minneapolis, 48 in St. Paul, 41 in Duluth, and 86 others throughout the state. The neighboring state of Wisconsin was home to 172 Chinese at this time.

Circumstances in China remained difficult, and many men sought means to support their families by seeking work abroad. Those individuals choosing to journey to the United States often entered the country as "paper sons or daughters." After decades of restrictive legislation, the rulings on derivative citizenship gave rise to the immigration slot racket, whereby Chinese merchants and Chinese American citizens in the United States falsely registered the births of children in China in order to create slots for future immigrants. The slots could later be sold to others who wanted to bring sons or daughters to the

United States but who did not have merchant or citizen status.[8]

Paper sons and daughters adopted new names prior to traveling to the United States. For example, before leaving China, a son from the Moy family took on the experiential memory of someone from the Chin family. Detailed coaching books provided information about the "adopted" family, including names, birthdays, addresses, physical attributes, and particulars about the home village so that the new arrival could persuade the Chinese inspectors that they were, indeed, who they claimed to be. Travel plans could be delayed or entry denied if an inspector was not satisfied with the applicant's answers.[9]

Since the Geary Act already required close monitoring of Chinese immigrants by immigration officials, newspapers turned their attention to eagerly watching over activities within the community. Often factual, sometimes racist, these articles provided glimpses into the Chinese community that were seldom documented for those immigrants whose physical appearance and mannerisms easily fit into mainstream Minnesota. Of particular interest to local newspapers were the dress and hairstyles of the Chinese. While many merchants adapted western dress as early as the 1890s, many Chinese laborers in Minnesota retained their traditional queues as was required by royal decree of the Ching dynasty. However, with changes in political power in China in 1910, Chinese laborers began to adapt western hair styles. A Minneapolis restaurateur noted in the October 24, 1911, edition of the *Minneapolis Journal,* "Minneapolis has a larger percentage of queueless and progressive Chinamen than any other large American city.... Minneapolis Chinese are rebels in spirit."

Newspapers reported on Chinese New Year's festivities annually, paying particular attention to never-before-heard-of foods and celebratory fireworks. Other articles often covered rites of passage and social events of leaders within the community, reflecting the successful efforts of these individuals to interact with and be respected by mainstream society.

Settlement in Minnesota

Between 1876 and 1910, Chinese businesses were generally located in downtown areas of Minnesota's larger cities and towns. While they did not constitute separate Chinatowns, they were close enough to each other to allow the formation of networks of mutual assistance and to provide for the social and material needs of the immigrants.

Chinese restaurants and stores appeared in greater numbers after the turn of the century. By 1910 there were ten Chinese restaurants in Minneapolis, and six each in St. Paul and Duluth. Early restaurants in the Twin Cities were often decorated with teakwood furniture and silk panels to attract visitors looking for an "exotic" experience, a word often used by publications to describe Chinese culture and

Woo Du Sing inspected merchandise in the store Yee Sing and Company, jointly owned with his brother Woo Yee Sing, located at 22 Western Ave., Minneapolis, about 1920.

Yuen Faung Low (John's Place)

Woo Yee Sing and his younger brother Woo Du Sing moved their restaurant several times before settling in at 28–30 6th St. S. in Minneapolis around 1904. Yuen Faung Low (translates as Exotic Fragrance from Afar), was also called John's Place, after a nickname given to Woo Yee Sing. It was known for an exquisite interior that featured carved wood, silk panels, and tables with mother-of-pearl inlay, as shown in this photograph from about 1915. The Woo brothers displayed a five-piece altar set in the dining area to bring good luck to their new business. Crafted specifically for the restaurant and purchased in Guangzhou in about 1910, the set consisted of two flower vases, two candle holders, and a tiered incense urn. Charles H. Woo and

Altar piece from the Woo brothers' restaurant

Howard F. Woo, sons of Woo Du Sing and Woo Yee Sing, respectively, managed the restaurant after the deaths of their fathers, aided by Lolita Woo (Howard's wife), Donald Woo (the son of the third Woo brother), and Jack Hong Jue (the son of the original chef). The restaurant catered mostly to downtown employees and shoppers. Originally serving mainly chow mein and chop suey, menu offerings were expanded after World War II as U.S. soldiers who had been stationed in China and had experienced more traditional flavors and ingredients began patronizing the restaurant. The building remained until 1967 when the Woo family lost its lease, and the building was torn down for a parking lot. At that time most of the restaurant's articles—from furniture to dishes—were sold, many to longtime customers.

Interior of
Yuen Faung Low,
about 1915

food. Restaurants usually served both American and Chinese food to accommodate a wide variety of palates. Like their counterparts in the laundry business, restaurant employees worked long days with business hours beginning as early as 10:30 A.M. and ending at 3:00 A.M. the following day. Proprietors and employees often resided in cramped quarters within the same space occupied by their businesses.

A small number of Chinese-owned grocery stores opened in St. Paul, Minneapolis, and Duluth in the early 1900s. These stores carried an assortment of items including rice, pottery, canned goods, groceries, clothing, Chinese herbs, and supplies needed by local laundries. These stores likely provided goods to Chinese businesses outside of the metro area and throughout the Upper Midwest.[10]

Following the completion of the transcontinental railroad from St. Paul to the West Coast in 1883, Chinese store owners may have begun serving as agents for local businessmen who engaged in trade with China, such as James J. Hill who initiated business negotiations as early as the 1870s. By 1901 Hill's Northern Pacific Steamship Company was transporting more than 44,000 tons of flour per year to Hong Kong, China, and Japan.[11]

Besides supplying local Chinese with goods from home, stores also served as a gathering place where men could share family news from China and get assistance with translations and sending money back home. Isolated from the larger society by barriers of language and culture, these stores provided a sense of community where one could be surrounded by familiar dress, food, and shared histories. The stores served as a home away from home where individuals were accepted for who they were rather than being diminished for who they were not.[12]

Family life developed slowly in Minnesota's early Chinese community and elsewhere in the United States, due to the restrictions of immigration law, Chinese tradition, and the high cost of trans-Pacific travel. Nevertheless at least

Chinese Store Inventory

In 1902 St. Paul businessman Moy Hee established a retail shop called Wing Wah Chong Merchandise Company, which specialized in silks, embroidered goods, rice, pottery, canned goods, groceries, and toys. The wide variety of wares available were typical of those carried by many such establishments. These stores provided supplies for local Chinese restaurants and laundries as well as the general public. The list below represents excerpts from an itemized statement of his property at the time of his death in 1921.

64 packages Oolong tea (⅓ pound)
16 packages Teng Yen tea (⅓ pound)
22 packages Look Wan tea (½ pound)
37 ironing pads
30 pairs grass slippers
38 bottles marking ink
29 books (6″ x 14″)
200 Chinese pencils
7 Chinese jackets
25 pair Chinese shoes
21 brass skimming spoons for chop suey
9 large size chop knife
17 cans lemon jelly
19 cans sour bamboo
12 bottles Stewarts bluing
27 cans candied ginger
35 cans cucumber bitter melon
32 cans lily root
50 cans pickled kohlrabi

6 cans Chinese white fish salt
38 bamboo brush, large
39 bamboo brush, small
8 lbs. dried sea weed
11 lbs. dried shrimp, small
25 lbs. imported dried noodle
100 pair Chinese cloth slipper
160 novelty tea pots
7 lbs. bean flour for oyster
1 keg thick soy sauce (100 lbs.)
14 kegs thin soy sauce (100 lbs.)
The following contained various Chinese
    drugs:
    7 one gallon glass museum jars
    35 one pint glass mason jars
    48 one quart glass mason jars
    133½ gallon glass mason jars
    24 stoneware jars, 3 gallon

This tea set was a gift from Moy S. James, cousin of Moy Hee and owner of St. Paul's Shanghai Café, to Julia Fink, the nurse who worked for his family in the 1910s. This "novelty" tea set is an example of the goods that may have been sold in Moy Hee's store.

An event that likely piqued the imagination of Minnesotans was the completion of the Northern Pacific Railway from St. Paul to the West Coast in 1883. To mark the occasion, a large celebration took place in the streets of St. Paul where a Chinese arch was built on Wabasha Street between Ninth and Tenth Streets. "The span of the arch was forty feet in length, . . .The center of the arch formed a unique pagoda; three stories in height, the roof was embellished with over two hundred Chinese lanterns." On the front side of the arch was the motto: "Northern Pacific Railroad connection between China and St. Paul."

six families were established in Minnesota before 1910. Since virtually all the early immigrants were men, these families were formed by marriages with Chinese women from the West Coast or China and by intermarriage with non-Chinese women. Mixed marriages were an integral

A number of Chinese men living in Minnesota chose non-Chinese brides as indicated in this wedding portrait of James Mar, a Chinese immigrant, and Julia A. Zyzner, a Polish American from Silver Lake. The couple was married at St. Vincent's Church in St. Paul on September 14, 1908. A note on the portrait stated that Mar was China's "first Catholic Convert in America, and now is [a] Lay Missionary to convert his countrymen in St. Paul and Minneapolis."

part of many early immigrant communities in Minnesota.[13]

In 1910 there were nine Chinese women living in Minnesota—three native and six foreign born. By 1920 the numbers increased to 60 females, 34 native and 26 foreign born. Wives of merchants, often educated and fluent in English, had more opportunities to interact with mainstream society. Chinese women of lesser means or having little knowledge of the English language likely led more isolated lives. Liang May Seen, wife of Woo Yee Sing, was from the West Coast and the first Chinese woman to settle in Minneapolis in 1892. She managed her own curio shop, attended the English-language services at Westminster Presbyterian Church, and served as an important role model for Chinese women in the Twin Cities until her death in 1946. In contrast, her sister-in-law, the wife of Woo Du Sing, had bound feet, spoke only Chinese, and seldom left her home.[14]

Chinese women also began settling across the river in St. Paul. One such individual was Judith Moy (Wong Shee), who arrived from China in 1904. Fluent in English, she was active in community organizations, was the first Chinese woman to be a member of any Christian church in St. Paul, and assisted customers at her husband's restaurant, Kwong Tung Low and Company, located at 413 Robert Street.[15]

Chinese families in Minnesota often socialized on Sundays, the only day of rest for most folks. Children from these families were enrolled in public schools, and many attended Bible study classes at local churches. Schools and churches also provided children with opportunities to participate in extracurricular activities, such as scouting and summer camps. Many children, however, found

In 1904 Moy Hee of St. Paul returned to China to marry Wong Shee (Judith Moy), a marriage arranged by his mother. After arriving in Vancouver, they traveled east by rail through Canada and entered the United States through Portal, North Dakota, eventually making their way to St. Paul.

acceptance difficult. Howard Woo, son of Woo Yee Sing, was confronted with racial taunts and name calling at both his elementary and high schools in the early 1900s. To counter such influences and to guarantee that children retained knowledge of Chinese culture and language, parents established evening classes as early as 1921. These classes were an important means of maintaining Chinese traditions while at the same time bridging the gap between first and second generations living in the United States.[16]

Members of the community took advantage of opportunities that would help them learn more about American

This unidentified Chinese boy was a participant in the "Open Your Heart" Community Fund Campaign in the Twin Cities in 1925. Chinese Americans often worked with the Red Cross and other organizations to raise funds for China, which experienced famine and political turmoil throughout much of the 20th century.

culture. Their efforts to do so were often assisted by organizations such as churches and YMCAs, both longtime supporters of missionary and charitable work in China. As early as 1882, churches throughout the state established English classes. These classrooms offered a familiar environment for Chinese who had attended mission schools back home. YMCAs in both Minneapolis and Duluth sponsored similar English classes during the late 19th and early 20th centuries.[17]

Unfortunate circumstances in China presented opportunities for Chinese to work with mainstream organizations in efforts to raise funds for relief from a famine that was devastating China. In 1912 the American Red Cross appointed Moy S. James and Charles Yenwah of Minneapolis and Gee Quak Wah of St. Paul to solicit funds. The committee successfully raised $388 for the cause. As other needs arose throughout the 20th century, Chinese Americans in the Twin Cities and Duluth coordinated similar fund-raising efforts for China.[18]

The Chinese were tireless in their efforts to become accepted into mainstream America, despite having their civil rights violated and being subjected to unjust ordinances. Between 1880 and 1900, the Chinese challenged unfair taxes and regulations by bringing some twenty appeals to the United States Supreme Court. As Charles J. McClain noted in his book *In Search of Equality*, "The United States, whatever its faults, was a country devoted to the rule of law." The Chinese were protected under a number of legal provisions, most notably the Fourteenth Amendment, and they applied this knowledge when seeking protection from the courts.[19]

Such action was evident in Minnesota as early as 1902 when cooks unions, faced with unfounded fears that Chinese threatened job security, picketed outside the entrances of Chinese restaurants in Minneapolis. As customers entered the restaurants, they received cards that read, "We, as union men, ask you to keep away from Chinese restaurants. They are unfair and a menace to white labor." Citing the Fourteenth Amendment, which guaranteed equal protection under the law, Woo Yee Sing, owner of the Canton Café, hired the law firm of Keith, Evans, Thompson, and Fairchild to proceed against union members. The courts ruled in Woo's favor and prohibited meddling union men from picketing on restaurant premises. Similar union protests took place in front of Chinese restaurants in Duluth in 1903.[20]

Early Chinese also used the legal system to challenge biased representations of their race and

This "Please Help" donation box was used in the Twin Cities in 1921 to raise money for the Chinese Relief Campaign, a national fund raiser to address the needs of famine-stricken China. According to the April 7, 1921, issue of the *Minnesota Alumni Weekly*, the University of Minnesota collected almost $5,000 for the cause.

In 1883 Woo Yee Sing and his younger brother Woo Du Sing opened the Canton Café, thought to be the first Chinese restaurant in Minnesota, on 1st Ave. S. in Minneapolis. By 1905, when this photograph was taken, the restaurant was located at 246–248 Marquette Ave.

culture. In 1919, St. Paul Chinese worked with members of the Twin Cities National Association for the Advancement of Colored People (NAACP) to draft a bill that would ban plays that created race hatred. This legal action was prompted by the showing of *The Midnight Patrol,* a "play depicting Chinese life in a western metropolis" that focused on alleged opium trade rather than the many positive contributions of individuals in Chinese communities. While 1919 Minnesota legislative records do not reflect successful passage of such a law, it is the first known collaborative protest involving Chinese and African Americans in the state to "support a sense of fair play and prejudice to none." Hollywood's stereotypical portrayals of Chinese continued in the 1920s and 1930s with the introduction of two new characters: Fu Manchu and Charlie Chan, both portrayed by white actors. Unfortunately, these movies influenced perceptions of many generations of Americans and only served to further already deeply rooted stereotypes of Chinese.[21]

While conflicts outside of the community were handled through the courts, disagreements among the Chinese themselves were, depending on the circumstances, managed in a variety of ways. Family and merchants associations served as employment and housing agencies, welcome wagons, and labor contractors. These organizations kept peace in the community by resolving conflicts within the family or the association or through programs within the framework of established churches and social agencies. Tongs, another type of association, began to appear in the Twin Cities in the 1910s. They drew their membership from businessmen who were largely immigrants from South China. Initially tongs served to protect members from encroachment by rival Chinese businessmen and provided fraternal support in factional quarrels. Tong organizations were almost exclusively found on the East and West Coasts, and while their numbers remained small in Minnesota, the press was eager to follow their every move.[22]

Members of the Hip Sing tong, an organization associated with the West Coast, made their presence known in 1912 when they threatened Twin Cities Chinese in order to extort monetary payments. In response, early leaders of the St. Paul Chinese community requested help from the governor to keep tongs out of the Twin Cities. Rumors of tong activity continued throughout the 1910s, and newspapers frequently reported on raids of local businesses although searches rarely produced the results promised in the dramatic headlines used to entice readers. Such actions often loomed larger in the minds of reporters than they did in the community. Newspapers also used the terms "tong" and "merchant associations" interchangeably,

Men and women gathered at an On Leong Association meeting hall decorated with U.S and China flags in Minneapolis, about 1925.

making it difficult for readers to distinguish between the two entities.[23]

On August 1, 1920, a Minnesota branch of the On Leong Chinese Merchant's Association was established at 318 3rd St. S., Minneapolis. Approximately 200 Chinese from around the country attended the convention where a $6,000 banquet and a Chinese orchestra commemorated the event. The August 1, 1920, *Minneapolis Journal* emphasized that "at the convention are many Chinese who have degrees from American colleges. Every delegate is a successful businessman."

This was a challenging time for business leaders such as Wong Wen who lived on the West Coast before moving to Minneapolis in 1912 where he worked at the Grand Restaurant and So Chu Inn. His wife and son in China joined him in Minnesota in 1921 and he opened his own restaurant, the Kin Chu Café, in 1923. As president of the On Leong, Wong was an important leader in the Chinese community in the 1920s and 1930s, protecting the businesses of the association's members. Wong sold the Kin Chu Café in 1961 and later opened the Kwong Tung Noodle Manufacturing Company. With official paperwork confirming that he was a native U.S. citizen, Wong took full advantage of his ability to vote and was an ardent supporter of Republican candidates, including Wendell Willkie in 1940 and Thomas E. Dewey in 1944.[24]

During the 1920s and 1930s, tensions escalated between the Hip Sing and On Leong organizations in several U.S. cities. Business leaders from San Francisco, New York, and Chicago served as mediators between the two national organizations and brokered a truce on March 26, 1925. Despite their efforts, conflicts continued into the 1930s. Tensions developed in Minneapolis due to claims that On Leong had total control of the Chinese restaurants located in St. Paul. Between October 1924 and October 1925, nine tong related shootings occurred in the Twin Cities. Unfortunately, the actions of a few only fueled unsubstantiated suspicions already overshadowing the Chinese American community.[25]

The intense scrutiny under which most Chinese lived was evident after the October 2, 1925, shooting of George Chin, a laundry owner at 614 7th St. S., Minneapolis. Mayor George E. Leach, Chinese Inspector Charles W. Seaman, and Police Chief Frank W. Brunskill responded by calling for a round-up of Minneapolis Chinese. Within two days, more than 150 Chinese—over a third of the city's Chinese population—had been arrested and put in jail. The majority of Chinese were able to produce certificates of residency (paperwork that showed that they had the right to remain in the United States) and were released that same day. Of the total arrested, nine admitted to being members of a tong. Within a few days, only two remained in jail from the roundup. Similar roundups took place in New York, Cleveland, and Boston.[26]

By the mid-1930s nationwide tong activity had come to a halt. Leaders recognized that such violence not only reinforced negative stereotypes of Chinese but also greatly affected the livelihood of Chinese business owners. Community efforts to send aid to China during the war against Japan may have also been a factor in the end to violent conflict between tongs. For the remainder of the 20th century, On Leong and Hip Sing functioned largely as social clubs and support networks for Chinese-owned businesses in Minnesota. While both the Hip Sing and On Leong organizations were based in the Twin Cities, out-state Chinese contributed money and maintained social ties with them. As job opportunities improved and new professional organizations emerged for Chinese Americans, membership in these organizations greatly declined in the latter part of the 20th century.[27]

In smaller cities and towns where immigrant associations were not organized locally, leadership was generally based on business success and property ownership, as well as education and age. For example, in the southern part of the state Chinese in Austin and Albert Lea formed a close-

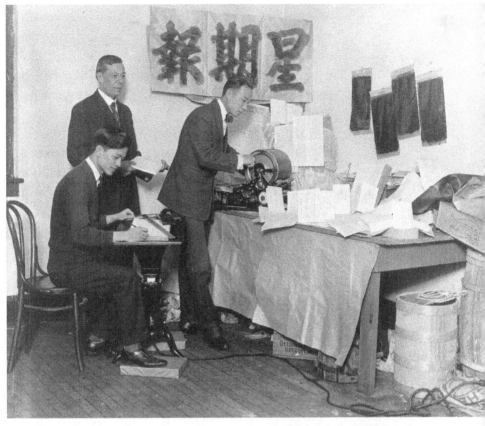

知星報

knit community through frequent movement between the towns. Sammy Wong and Wong Hong were leaders in that area, respectively, and both promoted good relations with local businessmen and police.[28]

Younger men who remained independent of business conflicts were also rising to important positions in the community during this period. One of these was Henry Yep, who, like Woo Yee Sing, favored interaction between the Chinese community and the dominant society. In Minneapolis he became a leader of Westminster Presbyterian Church's Sunday afternoon Chinese-language services. Like many of the independent leaders, Yep spoke both English and Chinese and frequently served as interpreter for new immigrants. Under his leadership Chinese members

Members of the Twin Cities Chinese community, under the leadership of Henry Yep, published a Chinese-language newspaper entitled *Sing Kee Po* (The Chinese Weekly) in the 1920s.

of Westminster Church, assisted by a Chinese student at Hamline University, published a Chinese-language newspaper entitled *Sing Kee Po* (The Chinese Weekly). Each 24-page issue included foreign news—particularly items concerning China—domestic news, and advertisements of Chinese businesses.

Kim Wah, popularly known as Walter C. James, was another neutral, independent leader who, like Woo and Yep, spoke both English and Chinese. Born in Yakima, Washington, James migrated to the Midwest as a young man in

the early 1900s. After first establishing a successful restaurant in Chicago, he moved to Minneapolis in 1909. There three years later he opened the Canton Grill in the basement of the Dyckman Hotel. In 1919 he established the Nankin Cafe on 7th Street South, a longtime favorite among Twin Cities residents until the restaurant closed in 1981. James was strongly committed to establishing close ties between the Chinese and the larger Twin Cities society; he was also concerned about the welfare of new immigrants. In order to serve better as liaison between the Chinese and other Minnesotans, he became an active member of the Rotary, the YMCA, and the Salvation Army.[29]

Walter James (Kim Wah), a longtime Minneapolis businessman and owner of the Nankin restaurant, was well known for his generosity within the Chinese American community.

While Chinese began new lives in Minnesota, they kept a watchful eye on unfolding events in China. Individuals were especially concerned for families and relatives back home. Unfair treaties with western nations had resulted in fierce anti-foreign riots in 1900 (the Boxer Rebellion) and, after thousands of people lost their lives, an army of troops from eight nations moved in to keep order. The Manchu (Ching) dynasty, in power since 1644, abdicated in 1911. Despite Sun Yat-sen's efforts to establish a democratic Chinese republic, a decade of rule by rival warlords followed.[30]

Entrepreneurs and political leaders from China often stopped in the Twin Cities to conduct meetings and provide updates regarding changes in China's political regime to fellow Chinese. While the population of the state's Chinese community was relatively small, a number of local leaders owned property in both China and the United States allowing them to flex their financial muscle and power in both arenas.[31]

An article appearing in the October 14, 1911, *Minneapolis Journal* described the response of local Chinese celebrating the successes of the revolutionary party in China. Minneapolis leader, Moy S. James, emphasized that "the Minneapolis and St. Paul Chinese are dropping old superstitions and customs and taking up the American ways . . . the readiness with which the Chinese cut their queues a year ago when the more modern Chinese began it, showed that the Twin Cities Chinese are progressive."

Chinese in Minnesota kept abreast of the political chaos that emerged after the demise of the Ching dynasty. When a weak Chinese government made concessions to Japan after World War I, nationalism soared, which presented Sun Yat-sen with another opportunity to revitalize the Nationalist Party or Kuomintang (KMT).

Support for the KMT in St. Paul was organized in early 1920. People met to learn of Sun Yat-sen's progress and raise money for his efforts. Under the leadership of Moy Hee, a Chinese Nationalist League office was established on the second floor of his dry goods store in St. Paul. Pictures of George Washington, Abraham Lincoln, and Woodrow Wilson decorated the walls. In February 1920 more than 100 representatives from Detroit, Milwaukee, Chicago, and Minneapolis attended a fund-raising dinner at 440 Wabasha St., St. Paul. Sam Wong, "a graduate of the Mechanic Arts High School," presided over the meeting. He emphasized the democratic ideals of the new Chinese Republic and also "urged Americanization among the Chinese."

This was the first and last known dinner held in St. Paul to support Sun Yat-sen's efforts. Most Chinese were not making enough money to provide funds for both the KMT and families back home. Also, in 1921, the KMT collaborated with the Chinese Communist Party to end the division of China into military regions run by warlords and the exploitation of privileged powers such as Britain, France, the United States, and Japan. The political powers and energies of China were moving in yet another direction.[32]

Wedged between Confucian ideals and discriminatory legislation, the Chinese continued to seek new opportunities and adventures in the United States. Their willingness to see beyond limitations and challenges imposed by powers outside their control provided them with the fortitude required to live a transnational existence.

The Pre–World War II Community

Minnesota's Chinese community experienced considerable population growth between the years 1910 and 1928. By 1920 approximately 500 Chinese were living in the state with the largest number, 300, residing in Minneapolis and St. Paul. By the late 1920s the Chinese population reached an estimated 900 to 1,000 people, including more than 100 women. The increase in numbers can be attributed to a number of factors.

As immigration laws grew increasingly restrictive for Chinese, earlier court decisions had affirmed the rights of merchants and American citizens to bring wives and children to the United States. By 1927 the courts had acknowledged the right of foreign-born children and grandchildren of American-born Chinese to derivative citizenship. Chinese families, almost non-existent at the turn of the century, were now visible throughout metropolitan and rural areas of Minnesota.

Family life began to develop more fully in the Chinese community during the 1910–39 period, although the population still consisted largely of men who were single or whose families lived in China. In the Twin Cities the number of families grew from about seven to thirty during this time period. Some families reached Minnesota on merchant papers, but the majority were formed by marriages of the second generation. Of the 24 sons and daughters of immigrants who settled in the state before 1910, many married Chinese from the West Coast. Others married local non-Chinese, forming about a half-dozen intermarried families in the Chinese American community prior to World War II. A few of the immigrants' daughters wed Chinese students attending the University of Minnesota, and a number of early

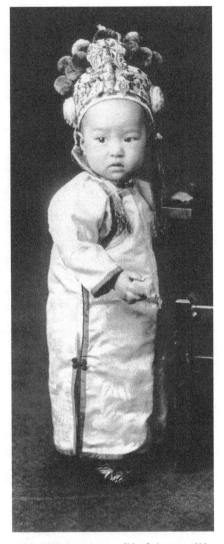

Archibald Moy was the son of Moy S. James and his wife Bessie, who operated Shanghai Low, a Chinese restaurant located on Wabasha Street in St. Paul in the early 20th century.

settlers' sons married wives from China. Most of the early immigrants' children remained in Minnesota after marriage, contributing to the development of Chinese family life there.

Tradition versus the Individual: Seong Moy

During the 1930s, children like Seong Moy were sent to the United States for an American education and to learn the restaurant business to support the family back home. Arriving in St. Paul in 1931, Seong attended grade school and worked with relatives at the Port Arthur Café on Robert Street. Moy persuaded his grandfather to allow him to attend high school if he would continue his apprenticeship at the restaurant. "Now of course being exposed to education, one tends to pick up many things which are sometimes contrary to the wishes of, let's say, an antiquated-thinking family. . . . For the first time I was beginning to exert myself as an individual." Seong had to balance traditional responsibilities—serving and supporting family both in the United States and China—while exploring the new-found possibilities suddenly available to him.

Seong Moy, *Lovers in Flight* (woodcut, 1953)

Moy discovered the Federal Art Project School in St. Paul and later studied under Cameron Booth at the St. Paul School of Art from 1936 to 1940. After serving in the U.S. armed services during the war, he completed his formal art education in New York under the renowned painter and teacher Hans Hoffman. Although Moy decided to pursue a career in art rather than the restaurant business, his work reflected strong ties to Chinese methods of drawing and calligraphy—methods probably learned in his Chinese grade school before journeying to the United States. Moy is considered to be among the most important American woodcut artists of modern time and has been a longtime resident of New York.

The prosperous national economy of the 1920s likely gave rise to the increased number of Chinese-owned businesses in Minnesota. Minneapolis, the largest Chinese settlement in the state, saw laundries increase from 23 in 1910 to 73 in 1928 and restaurants from 10 to 23 during this same time period. St. Paul and Duluth experienced similar trends. New businesses required new employees, and

Members of the Huie family posed for a formal portrait in China prior to immigrating to Minnesota in 1928. The father, Huie Jock Jyao, lived in the United States for several years before bringing his family to Minnesota. From left to right: Huie Hung Wah (Phil) (middle son), Huie Yuen Shee (mother), Huie Jock Jyao, and Huie Hung Sing (Wing) (oldest son). Wing remained in China with his wife but later came to the United States as a paper son.

This family portrait was taken the same year that the Huie family immigrated from China. Quickly adapting to western dress, the Huie family announced the arrival of their daughter, Huie Quee Mee (Mae).

Chinese students attending the University of Minnesota, Twin Cities, were transported to the Midwest by the Great Northern Railroad. This photograph is from a 1925 promotional booklet touting the benefits of the Minnesota–China connection.

merchants likely brought over paper sons to assist with the demands of laundries and restaurants.[33]

During these years, China was experiencing political upheaval, civil wars, and famine. According to the records of Charles W. Seaman, Chinese inspector, fewer Twin Cities Chinese made return trips to China in 1925 than in any previous year. Seaman noted that an average of 40 of the 500 Chinese in St. Paul and Minneapolis had previously returned to China each year.[34]

Beginning in 1914 a small number of students from China enrolled at the University of Minnesota, adding another element to the growing Chinese community in the Twin Cities. The arrival of Chinese students marked the beginning of a long and significant relationship between the university and the country of China. The establishment of University of Minnesota alumni in China over the next 90 years greatly influenced the development of research, scholarship, and trade between China and Minnesota. Several other colleges and universities throughout Minnesota also have a long history of cultural and educational exchanges with China.

Early students studied agriculture, focusing on improving their country's food production, as well as mining and engineering. Despite class, regional, and language differences—most students spoke northern dialects, while immigrants spoke Cantonese or the dialects of *Sze Yup*—they regularly visited settlers' homes and socialized with their children. During this period a number of the immigrants' sons and daughters also began to enter the University of Minnesota, where they often found common interests with the students from China.

During the late 1920s and early 1930s, an average of five Chinese students arrived at the University of Minnesota each year. In 1934 this figure jumped to 15 and continued at more than 20 until the Japanese invaded China in 1937. After that, the number of new students dropped to a dozen or fewer each year up to World War II. Of the 63 students who entered the university during the 1936–40 period, 43 were enrolled in the College of Agriculture, with a focus on entomology and plant pathology. While a few remained in the United States after graduation, the majority returned to China. Many of these professionals led the postwar agricultural reconstruction programs in both the People's Republic of China and Taiwan.[35]

Immigration from China came to a virtual standstill during the Depression years of the 1930s throughout the United States. As growing numbers of white Americans were thrown out of work, there was less money to pay for services Chinese provided, such as restaurants or laundries. In Minnesota some Chinese closed their shops and returned to their homeland. By 1935 laundries and restaurants decreased in numbers throughout the state, sometimes by as much as 50% in some cities.[36]

The Chinese Art Shoppe (Kim Wah Co.) at 57 9th St. S. in Minneapolis, about 1926, was owned by Selma F. James.

Restaurants in less-populated areas, such as the O.K. Café in St. Cloud, managed to stay in business despite the poor economy. Owner Eddy Wong and family members kept the restaurant open twelve hours a day, seven days a week. A stuffed owl with bloodshot eyes was displayed in the restaurant in the 1930s to symbolize that employees of the O.K. Café appeared never to sleep.[37]

Other businesses, such as the Chinese Gift Shop in

Minneapolis, attracted new customers by offering mah-
jong lessons, a popular game in the 1930s. In addition to
selling imported Chinese giftware, husband and wife team
Stanley and Marvel Chong worked with buyers in China to
purchase antiques to sell in their store. In 1944 the Chongs
established the International House of Foods, a successful
wholesale and retail business specializing in Asian foods
and restaurant supplies that met the needs of restaurants
throughout the Midwest.[38]

During the 1920s and 1930s, Minnesota continued to
provide a more tolerant and accepting environment toward the Chinese than did other areas of the country although discrimination was still prevalent in the job and
housing markets. Lolita Woo, chief cook at Yuen Faung
Low (John's Place) for many years, recalled her surprise
when attending her first movie in Minneapolis in 1931

Westminster Presbyterian Church, Minneapolis, was an important anchor for the Chinese community beginning in the 1880s. Events such as this bazaar in the mid-1930s helped raise funds for ongoing support of
the Chinese program at the church.

after relocating from Oregon. It marked the first time in her life that she was ushered down the center aisle of a theater rather than being restricted to the side aisles. This simple but important gesture significantly affected her perception of possibilities within her new surroundings.[39]

While the majority of Chinese still worked for Chinese-owned businesses in the 1930s, a small number of individuals found employment with other agencies including Duluth shipyards, engineering firms, and offices. By the 1930s many Chinese Americans had college degrees, but discrimination limited the ability of employers to view them as competent hires. A number of educated American-born Chinese (ABCs) looked to China as a more viable option to grow professionally although it hindered their ability to address underlying questions of identity and allegiance. Nationally, one in five ABCs migrated to work in China and found employment at foreign branches of U.S. corporations, government agencies, or educational institutions. Many returned to the United States after a few years as the threat of war in China became a reality.[40]

World War II and the Postwar Era

By the beginning of World War II, the Chinese population in the United States had dwindled to 78,000. However Chinese Americans were eager to demonstrate their support for the United States, and nearly 20% of Chinese adult males enlisted or were drafted into the armed services. The enlistment average for the general population was 8.6%.[41]

The participation of Chinese in both military and civilian efforts during World War II represented the first time the community took part in a major activity of the larger society. Twin Cities merchants turned their attention to the sons of Chinese immigrants, who were training at the War Department's Military Intelligence Service Language

Fort Snelling Military Intelligence Service Language School

During World War II, sons of Chinese immigrants trained at the War Department's Military Intelligence Service Language School (MISLS) at Camp Savage and later at Fort Snelling. These young men were organized as students in training companies and were later assigned to specific units upon graduation. The division director was First Lieutenant Ernest K. H. Eng, and Staff Sergeants included Wong Kan, Frank Chen, and Yuk Ow.

In 1945 the regiment compiled a Fort Snelling Memoir Book in which the young men recorded their experiences. Woven into their memories were the many visits to Twin Cites Chinese restaurants where owners organized recreational programs, holiday celebrations, and special Chinese meals and did their best to make the young men feel at home.

December 6, 1944, all the things that happened before then ... the tar-paper shacks ... a handful of men that was slow to increase ... the monotonous routine of CQ and KP, CQ and KP ... the coal stoves, and cooking chow mein with la chang and scalding tea on them ... dodging details ... hanging storm windows. ... And the bitter cold ... the rumors that changed with the wind ... and the slow, hardly perceptible increase of Chung Kuo Jen from a squad to a platoon ...

Christmas Eve party at Westminster. .. Santa Claus served egg-nog at John's ... New Year's 1945 ... terrific party at Nanking ... courtesy Mr. James ... plenty of liquor ...

No rest for the weary the work continues to increase ... no longer am sure whether the squad room is part of the barracks or just a front for a gambling den ... wherever you turn it's either marching, tien-kow or just plain poker ... hoi pei, hoi pei all day long ...

Wednesday night—the only day for play ... Hip Sing plays host ... huge banquet.

... familiar command—"Double time-march" ... for Quartermaster, he's a tough Joe ... starting to depend entirely on Chow Fan for nourishment ... chow in camp stinks ... thank God for Port Arthur ...

Chinese New Year's ... two day holiday ... big time at John's Place ... everybody there ... wine, women and song without end ... Fen soup with all of the fixings ...

Everything in blossom ... guests at University picnic ... big fried rice party to celebrate promotions ... thirteen of them to be exact ... parties sponsored by the officers ... Tom Poy and his dramatic presentation of Chinese operas ... talent scout gives Kim Wong, Shek Wong and Big Lee the once over ... as usual ... rumors ... will it be ship or plane? ... do we get more promotions or do we get busted? ... plans being made for farewell party ...

A group of soldiers relaxed around a table with mother-of-pearl inlay at John's Place.

The U.S. Government Printing Office issued posters like this during World War II when the United States allied with China to defeat enemy forces.

School (MISLS). Chinese businessmen also provided aid to students from China who were stranded in Minnesota by the war and cut off from supporting funds.[42]

For many Chinese, it was the first time that they worked side by side with whites in the work force. Whether retrofitting airplanes at Holman Field in St. Paul or working as engineers for companies awarded government contracts, never-before job opportunities and higher salaries were suddenly made available to the Chinese, despite the fact that many of them had held college degrees prior to the war.

The Chinese experienced a significant rise in popularity during World War II and were promoted as "friends" on posters and propaganda materials. One means of honoring this new found friendship was the creation of "victory" pins ornamented with small, colorful renditions of U.S. and China flags. Ostensibly to show support for the war and to celebrate the nation's alliance with China, the pins were to be worn by Chinese so that others could distinguish them from those of Japanese descent. While support for the Chinese community was a welcomed occurrence, it was unfortunate that it also signified the transfer of racism from one Asian American community to another.[43]

Beyond their display of patriotism, the Chinese were also concerned about their families in China. The Toishan region, the point of origin for most of the Chinese living in the United States, was particularly hard hit as village crops were used to feed Japanese troops. The situation worsened in 1941 when Hong Kong was captured by Japan, and the flow of U.S. money to relatives in southern China was cut off.[44]

The community initiated many national efforts to make the public aware of China's plight. Starting in 1938, San Francisco's Chinatown organized "Rice Bowl" parties— mardi gras style street festivals—to raise money and supplies for the Nationalist Party. Chinese in the Twin Cities and Duluth arranged several fund raisers to support Chinese back home. One such event was the Bowl of Rice dinner, held in 1941 at the Shrine Auditorium in Duluth. Fifty members of the Duluth Chinese community prepared and served the dinner for more than 1,000 people. All of the proceeds went to support the American Bureau for Medical Aid to China.[45]

Chinese Americans wore "victory" lapel pins during World War II. This one was worn by Harry Chin, who was employed as a cook in several Twin Cities Chinese restaurants.

The largest effort, however, went into the organization of the Twin Cities Chinese Emergency Relief Society to raise money for civilian relief funds and military supplies to be sent to China. In 1941 alone the group raised $45,000 for relief and $20,000 for military aid in the small Twin Cities Chinese community of about 400 people. According to an article in the March 23, 1941, *Minneapolis Star Journal,* three Chinese businessmen headed a relief committee that required every employed Chinese to contribute money each month. "Backsliders are almost unknown, and none escapes contributing his share in the end," the newspaper reported; an enforcement committee "makes certain that the individual does not fail in his duty to the group. Fines are imposed on delinquents."

Beginning in 1943, Walter Judd, newly elected U.S. Representative from Minnesota, urged Congress to repeal the Chinese Exclusion Act. Judd, having spent many years in China as a missionary, called on Congress to not only repeal the act but also to make Chinese eligible for naturalization and to allot annual immigration quotas allowing a total of 105 Chinese immigrants per year. Realizing how this discriminatory legislation against Chinese was an embarrassment to the United States during its wartime alliance with China, President Franklin D. Roosevelt called for an end to the Exclusion Act in December 1943. More importantly to Judd, the repeal of the Chinese Exclusion Act was an important step in Chinese Americans being treated as equals. He continued to support the efforts of Chinese Americans in Minnesota while in office for the next twenty years.[46]

The first two native Chinese in Minnesota to seek American citizenship with the clerk of the U.S. District Court were Marie Ling (Chin Sau Kin) and Harold Chin Kee—both from St. Paul. According to the July 21, 1944, *St. Paul Dispatch* "only two Chinese have been made citizens here—one a Chinese serving in the American army and the other born in China of American-Chinese parentage." Both the International Institute in St. Paul and the Council of Americanization in Minneapolis provided English classes and assisted the Chinese in preparing for citizenship.

Despite this progress, the Chinese still faced discrimination in the labor force. As late as 1943, some leaders in American labor unions still supported the Chinese Exclusion Act of 1882. The Minnesota Governor's Interracial Commission Report of 1949 found that in checking with the representatives from the hotel and restaurant unions no record of membership on the part of any Chinese was found. One Chinese employee in a Minneapolis restaurant said that he had once belonged to union in Chicago but had dropped out because he felt that the organization failed to gain the same benefits for him that it strove to get for its white members.[47]

After the war, Congress passed a number of bills to facilitate family reunification. The first, enacted on August 9, 1946, exempted Chinese wives of American citizens from quota restrictions and gave the wives of resident aliens preferential treatment within the quota. The second, on July 22, 1947, lifted the racial restrictions from the War Brides Act of 1945 and allowed approximately 8,000 Chinese women to enter the United States before it expired on December 30, 1949. Under the Refugee Relief Act of 1953, 2,000 Chinese were permitted entry, and several thousand living in the United States on temporary visas became eligible for permanent resident status.[48]

After World War II, Chinese-owned laundries diminished in number because a strong postwar economy allowed for more Americans to purchase washers and dryers. The reduced demand for laundries meant that entry level positions were not as easily available. Since education was deemed important for future success, many Chinese supported their children's efforts to attend college by establishing their own carryout businesses. Chinese Americans

The Poy Moy Hand Laundry, located at 471 St. Peter St. in St. Paul, was one of the few Chinese laundries remaining in Minnesota in the early 1960s.

who served in the military were eligible for benefits associated with GI bills, including low interest rates to purchase homes and pay for an education.

English and Bible study classes continued at Westminster Presbyterian Church into the 1950s. Many Chinese attending classes at Westminster had previously been students at mission schools in Guangdong province. Attendance increased after World War II when Chinese American soldiers traveled to China and returned with

Maurice Moy (Moy Gan Nai) purchased this well-established St. Paul restaurant in 1922. Previously known as Kwong Tung Low, Port Arthur remained a popular spot in downtown especially during the St. Paul Winter Carnival when the restaurant was filled to capacity. In this photograph taken in 1945 two Port Arthur delivery cars wait outside the restaurant to deliver take-out orders. The restaurant remained in business until 1957 when the building was razed.

Recent Chinese immigrants, including wives of Chinese American servicemen, attended an English-language class at Westminster Presbyterian Church, about 1950.

brides. In the fall of 1948 over a dozen young wives of Chinese American servicemen approached L. Jane Wilson, the superintendent of the Chinese Sunday school. They inquired about the possibility of starting English-language classes as well as Sunday afternoon religious programs geared to the special needs of the new arrivals. The classes also served as a support group for the war brides during a period of difficult adjustment.[49]

In 1950, Wilson reported that 25 to 30 families participated in classes offered by Westminster. Chinese American families enrolled in the church's programs were growing by leaps and bounds, and by 1950 there were 20 babies under the age of three. The friendships formed with other Chinese American children at Sunday school were crucial to the development of their Chinese American identity.[50]

The end of the Exclusion Era did not guarantee easy entry into the United States. Chinese wanting to enter the country were still confronted with bureaucratic complexi-

ties, endless paperwork, and delays. Jane Wilson wrote countless letters and made many phone calls to politicians, including Senator Hubert H. Humphrey, on behalf of her students and their families. The Chinese would later support Humphrey's campaign efforts in gratitude for his assistance to the community.[51]

Children posed with Chinese School Superintendent Jane Wilson (center) in the Westminster church refectory in the early 1950s.

After the war, an already devastated China was now faced with intense political struggles between Nationalist and Communist forces. As the Chinese Nationalist government confronted defeat in 1948–49, hundreds of thousands of people, mainly from Guangdong province, Shanghai, and other commercial centers, fled to Hong Kong. Concerned with crowded and unpredictable living conditions, Chinese living in the United States were frantic to get their relatives here. By the spring of 1950, the population of Hong Kong had swelled to an estimated 2.2 million, an increase of 1.5 million people in under five years. Following the establishment of Communist rule in 1949, the number of new arrivals from China dwindled, but immigration from Taiwan and Hong Kong continued. Between the early 1940s and 1960, Minnesota's Chinese population more than doubled to approximately 1,270.[52]

It is estimated that by 1949 about 100 Chinese American families were residing in the Twin Cities. For a number of years, Twin Cities leaders like Walter James and Stanley Chong encouraged socialization within the Chinese community. Chinese families often gathered at the Nankin restaurant or at the farmstead on Lake Howard owned by James. This social network evolved into the Chinese American Club in 1949, with the additional purpose of establishing a more formal presence within the Twin Cities Chinese community.[53]

The Chinese Dragon restaurant in Grand Rapids, about 1960. Chinese restaurants continued to have a presence in Minnesota throughout the 20th century and into the 21st.

The organization's newsletter, *The Communicator,* included announcements of births, marriages, graduations, trips, newly established businesses, and visits from other Chinese families living throughout the state, including Hibbing, Albert Lea, and Mankato. The club offered mother and baby courses in cooperation with the Red Cross. Members of the club participated in the Festival of Nations and operated the Zion Hall food hall at the Minnesota State Fair. The club often organized events like picnics and Thanksgiving dinners with Westminster Presbyterian Church. The Chinese Student Club at the University of Minnesota also participated in club events and in return invited members to dinner parties to celebrate the anniversary of the double 10 (establishment of the Chinese Republic on October 10, 1911).[54]

The Chinese American Club was open to all new immigrants, but its programs were designed primarily for those from southern China who identified with the Twin Cities Chinese business community. Some northern intellectuals and political refugees—and a few southern professionals—joined a student Bible study group formed in 1949, which was later named the Chinese Christian Fellowship in 1958. While the primary purpose of the fellowship was religious, it also served as an ethnic support group. When there were more families, it provided a Chinese-language school and other programs for religious and cultural instruction of the children as well.[55]

A 1950 directory published by the Chinese American Club noted the existence of the following organizations in the community: Chinese American Club, Chinese Community Club, Chinese Student Christian Association, Chinese Student Club, Chinese Sunday School, Hip Sing Association, On Leong Merchants Association of Minnesota, Wong Family Association, and the Moy Family Association. Businesses other than restaurants or laundries included the International House, Ming Importing Company, Mun

Hing Manufacturing Co., Peking Food Products Co., Thom's Chinese Gift Shop, and Wing Sang Lung Co.

Two years later the Chinese American Club evolved into the Chinese American Civic Council. Again led by Chong and James, the club dedicated "itself to the strengthening of those constructive social forces which create unity and understanding between the Chinese in America and other cultural and racial groups in the Midwest and to the steady development of sound public opinion which respects the rights of all citizens, regardless of race, creed or color."[56]

Post-World War II leadership within the Duluth Chinese community was guided by several businessmen, one of them being Joe Huie, a resident of Duluth since 1909. He emerged as the most prominent member of the immigrant community in the 1950s and 1960s. Born in Guangdong province in 1892, Huie worked in Duluth restaurants for six years before returning to his wife and son in China. He stayed for over a year, then went back to Duluth until 1933, when he again sailed for Guangzhou, where he opened a pharmaceutical outlet in 1946. He fled the city after the Communists established control and returned to Duluth with his two oldest sons in 1951.

In 1954 the rest of his family followed. Over the years Huie worked as dishwasher, cook, or manager in several Duluth restaurants before opening Joe Huie's Cafe in 1951. He gained prestige in the Chinese community through his business success, and as a Chinese leader gave generously to civic causes, including scholarships for students at the University of Minnesota–Duluth. He continued to work 16-hour days as manager, cashier, cook, and waiter until his retirement in 1973 at the age of 81. He also provided employment in his restaurant and developed a reputation as a practitioner of folk medicine.[57]

Following the takeover of mainland China (now referred to as the People's Republic of China or PRC) by Communist forces in 1949, Chinese Americans once again

found themselves in a precarious position. With the end of the Exclusion Era, Chinese obtained the right to see themselves as part of the nation's greater framework, as Americans. Despite this new identity, however, it was clear that their treatment remained linked to global politics and United States–China relations. The beginnings of the Cold War created irreconcilable differences between the two recently allied forces. The outbreak of war in Korea exacerbated the situation; this time the U.S. and China were on

Joe Huie stood in front of his restaurant on Lake Street in Duluth, about 1965.

The Huie family had five children with only the youngest being born in the United States. Lee Ngooh Kim Huie and her son Wing Young Huie relaxed in their Duluth home, about 1959.

opposite sides. Once again young Chinese American men entered the U.S. armed forces.

Leaders in the Chinese community were concerned that the war in Korea and Cold War propaganda would affect Chinese living in America. Their prophecies came true. Just as in the late 19th century, politicians began to make unfair charges against the entire Chinese community. Everett F. Drumwright, consul in Hong Kong, implied that

Ying Huie of Duluth served in the army during the Korean War.

Chinese Americans supported U.S. military efforts during the Korean War. Herbert Ling, a military draftee from St. Paul, gathered with his family (left to right), Mrs. Edward Chun, Marie Ling, Herbert Ling, Raymond Chung, and Mary Ling.

a network of Chinese spies had been established throughout the United States. The federal government instituted investigations of thousands of Chinese Americans, many of whom came to the United States as paper sons. The government created a "confession" program, implemented in 1955, that required those admitting their paper-son status to disclose fully their false documentation and to name relatives and friends who helped them. This measure created an atmosphere of distrust and caused a great deal of personal anguish within Chinese American families. Approximately 30,000 Chinese Americans confessed in order to legalize their citizenship status. Immigrants who had escaped corrupt politicians in China were now silenced by government authority in the United States.[58]

During the immediate postwar period, 300 to 400 Chinese students from the People's Republic of China, Taiwan, and Hong Kong attended the University of Minnesota. Following the wartime rupture in United States–China relations in 1950, the number of students from China declined considerably. Throughout the McCarthy era, surveillance by the Federal Bureau of Investigation of Chinese organizations at the university caused Chinese student activities to break down as members tried to keep a low profile. Many moved to the East and West Coasts to join the larger Chinese populations there; others returned to China.[59]

For the duration of the Cold War, student exchanges with mainland China ceased altogether. Students from Taiwan, however, continued to enroll at the university throughout this time and in 1952 established a nonprofit student organization known as the Minnesota Chinese Student Association. The MCSA continued to serve students from Taiwan and introduce Chinese culture to Minnesotans in 2003.[60]

Despite renewed suspicions and questioning they endured, members of the Chinese community persisted in

Ten Chinese students in agriculture were greeted by Fowler McCormick, president of the International Harvester Company, in 1945. Five of the students attended the University of Minnesota while the other five went on to Iowa State College.

their efforts to integrate into and be accepted by mainstream Minnesota. More and more professional opportunities were made available to them in the 1950s and 1960s. Chinese restaurants continued to thrive with more than 50 eateries in the Twin Cities alone while the once-ubiquitous laundries became a rare sight.[61]

Two examples of leading professionals within the community at this time were Joe Ling and Feng Hsiao. Ling, born in China in 1919, came to pursue graduate studies at the University of Minnesota in 1948. Four years later, he received the university's first doctorate in sanitary engineering. After returning to China for a few years, Dr. Ling and his wife, Rose (a research chemist), came back to Minnesota, and he went to work at 3M as the company's first engineer with a doctorate. Joe Ling became a near-legendary figure at 3M, having guided the company in the environmentally conscious 1970s toward a policy of pollution prevention in order to reduce production costs and energy needs. In 1999, he was named one of the 125 most important engineers of the last 125 years by *Engineering News-Record* magazine.[62]

Feng Hsiao was born in Shaanxi province in China. In 1945 he left China to pursue an advanced degree in engineering at the Massachusetts Institute of Technology. Two years later, he enrolled at the University of Minnesota. He left the university in 1949 to work full time for the Orville E. Madsen construction company, where he eventually became vice president and took the name of Fred Shaw for his business dealings. In 1974, Fred Feng Hsiao and Lyle Lundquist formed their own construction company, Shaw-

Fred and Jennie Hsiao were married in Minneapolis on June 6, 1958.

Lundquist Associates, Inc., which by 2003 was the largest minority-owned business in the Midwest.[63]

The Community at Midcentury

Beginning in the 1960s, a sizable number of second-generation Chinese, largely children of the postwar immigrant group and friends from Westminster Presbyterian classes, also entered the University of Minnesota and other colleges. In an era of active protest against the Vietnam War and increased ethnic consciousness, this group became highly politicized. Those at the university, along with a number of second-generation Japanese, were instrumental in establishing the Asian American Alliance. The first local pan-Asian student organization, the alliance provided a base for the developing ethnic consciousness of the second generation in the immigrant community. The group conducted education workshops for high school and college teachers, and their contact with black and Hispanic students culminated in the Color Brigade Unit, a group that marched from the university to the state capitol to protest the Vietnam War.[64]

As the Twin Cities Chinese population became larger and more diversified in the 1950s and 1960s, a sharp division occurred between southern Chinese businessmen and northern Chinese intellectuals. The southerners formed a close-knit social structure of family name associations, church programs, and educational clubs. The northerners—with the exception of those who belonged to the Chinese Christian Fellowship—were more loosely organized in small, intimate groups of friends that evolved out of the Chinese Student Association at the University of Minnesota. When concern grew over the deepening frictions within the community, Chinese leaders agreed to establish an umbrella association in which northerners, southerners, students, professionals, and businessmen could be brought together. About 1968 the Chinese American Club was renamed the Chinese American Association of Minnesota (CAAM), with unification of the community as its primary goal. Northern professionals asked longtime business leader Stanley Chong to serve as president to demonstrate their support for ongoing solidarity among members.[65]

The most important event in Chinese American history of the last fifty years was the signing on October 3, 1965, of the Immigration and Nationality Act. In place of quotas based on national origin, the new law substituted a preference system designed to reunify families and admit people who had needed skills. The act greatly increased the number of immigrants from Asia, especially Chinese from Taiwan and Hong Kong.

Taiwanese, many of whom had been forced to leave the mainland as children, began to arrive in Minnesota after World War II. By 1960, about 32 students from Taiwan were studying in the Twin Cities. Six years later, they founded the Formosan American Club of Minnesota, which soon evolved into the Taiwanese Association of America-Minnesota Chapter. The Taiwanese community grew from about 100 people some 35 years ago to several hundred people in 2002. Since 1979, the Taiwanese Association has represented Taiwan and its culture at the annual Festival of Nations sponsored by the International Institute of Minnesota.[66]

By the 1970s, Chinese immigrants were arriving from several different areas of Asia and establishing themselves throughout the metropolitan area. As a result, the community became more fragmented as distinct geographical affiliations and dialects were layered upon American, Chinese, Chinese American, or Asian American identities. This was a significant change from 100 years earlier when almost all Chinese immigrants arriving in Minnesota came from a small area in Guangdong province and lived within the boundaries of the downtowns.

The number of Chinese families living in the Twin Cities increased to 200 with a total state population of approximately 2,400 by 1970. Of this number, 50% were under 18 years of age, and about 30% were born between 1960 and 1970. The number of individuals in professional occupations in the Twin Cities represented over 30% of the metropolitan area's Chinese population compared to 18% nationally, in large part due to the business and educational climate of Minnesota.

In addition to the Chinese American community, there were a large number of Chinese students coming to the Twin Cities to study. By 1970

Taiwanese in Minnesota

全美台灣同鄉會明州分會

FORMOSAN CLUB OF MINNESOTA

The Taiwanese issued this brochure in 1977 to provide background information about their organizations and activities in Minnesota well as on the history of Taiwan.

there were about 400 Chinese students, most of them enrolled in graduate schools and living in the metropolitan area. They came from Taiwan, Hong Kong, and other parts of Southeast Asia as few students from the People's Republic of China were allowed to study abroad. The PRC, a country besieged by ever-changing reform movements and famine, remained cut off from the rest of the world.[67]

The Exclusion Law era effectively delayed the political mobilization of the Chinese for almost 70 years, but the Chinese community as a whole became more involved in local and national politics in the 1970s. Upon his return to Minnesota in 1971, Weiming Lu, a civil engineering graduate of the University of Minnesota, was struck by the community's almost nonexistent political voice and overall isolation from Chinese elsewhere in the nation. In the early 1970s he established the Minnesota Chapter of the Organization of Chinese Americans, a nonprofit advocacy group that encouraged legislative and policy initiatives at all levels of government to ensure the rights of Chinese and Asian American citizens. The Minnesota chapter addressed political issues and supported political candidates who "had an open attitude and were fair minded." Early efforts included raising money for George Latimer's campaign for governor in the Democratic-Farmer-Labor primary in 1986. Latimer later worked with Weiming Lu to establish a St. Paul Sister City in Changsha, China, in 1987.[68]

Chinese contributed generously to Hubert H. Humphrey's senatorial campaigns and supported Donald M. Fraser's Minneapolis mayoral campaign in 1979. The Chinese Chamber of Commerce also made a significant contribution to the Hubert H. Humphrey Institute of Public Affairs at the University of Minnesota, established in honor of the late senator in 1978. Humphrey had long been considered a friend of the Minnesota Chinese because of his frequent assistance with immigration problems. Many also supported his pro-Taiwan position.[69]

In 1970 CAAM organized all the Chinese groups to participate in the annual Aquatennial celebration in Minneapolis, the theme of which was "Seas of the Orient." An arch constructed by Fred Feng Hsiao was erected on Nicollet Avenue. Department store windows contained displays of Chinese arts and crafts. The program included a parade with floats and performances of the lion and sword dances and the martial arts. Walter James provided funds to pay travel expenses for the well-known St. Mary's High School girls drum corps from San Francisco's Chinatown to take part in the festivities.

The St. Mary's Chinese Girls Drum Corps gathered beneath the arch in downtown Minneapolis during the Aquatennial in 1970. After the festivities, the arch was moved to the state fairgrounds, where it stood until the 1990s.

Despite this show of unity, the goals of the business community and those of the professionals were basically divergent, and tensions soon arose within the new organization. While the businessmen wanted to promote commercial success, the intellectuals were more interested in sponsoring scholarships, dinners, and other social events. The conflict reached a climax during discussions of whether the Minnesota Chinese community should participate in the national Miss Chinatown contest in 1970. Businessmen saw potential economic gains in such an event, while the professionals looked upon it with distaste. The latter eventually agreed to go along with the contest, with the

understanding that those parents who did not favor beauty pageants would not permit their children to participate. The Miss Chinatown competition was held in Westminster Church with five candidates backed by various interest groups in the business community. The winner, Linda Shen, was feted in gala Minneapolis celebrations; she then went on to win the Miss Chinatown U.S.A. title the following year in San Francisco. After the local contest, the businessmen broke away from CAAM and formed the Chinese Chamber of Commerce.[70]

The divisions within the community were addressed in the preface of the 1970 *Chinese Community Directory,* published by CAAM. "We are living in a changing and a revolutionary world. In America the revolutionary spirit affects the social patterns. The Chinese in America, though indeed a minority group, are nevertheless a part of the greater society. This means that the Chinese community is also in the process of changing. The pioneer Chinese in the Twin Cities laid a solid foundation and gained a good reputation in the community. We should follow the footsteps of the pioneers, increase co-operation among ourselves, further the rich heritage of our culture and continually make contributions to the whole community!"

Several organizations made concerted efforts to support and maintain Chinese culture and language classes in the 1970s. Toisan or Cantonese classes were conducted by the Chinese Chamber of Commerce and taught at Westminster Presbyterian Church. Mandarin, a northern Chinese dialect, classes were offered by CAAM and the Chinese Christian Fellowship Church in Lauderdale, located midway between St. Paul and Minneapolis.[71]

In February 1972, President Richard Nixon traveled to Beijing for a historic meeting with Chairman Mao Zedong. After a quarter century of hostility between the two countries, repercussions from this meeting were significant. The United Nations recognized the People's Republic of China, the United States withdrew military support from Taiwan, and the U.S. began cultivating trade with the PRC. For the first time since 1949, contacting family and friends in the PRC was once again a possibility for Chinese living in America.[72]

Nixon's visit prompted immediate interest about all things Chinese including cooking. Two women from the Chinese community served as food ambassadors to Minnesota's general populace. Marvel Chong, who attended the University of Minnesota from 1927 to 1931, offered cooking classes in the evenings and hosted a call-in cooking show on Twin Cities radio station WCCO. At this time Marvel and her husband, Stanley, owned Marvel Frozen Foods, a wholesale food business that specialized in the production of packages of "Marvel Chow Mein" that were sold in stores throughout the Midwest. The Chongs were also responsible for introducing a new food item at the Minnesota State Fair in the 1960s. For 25 cents, Minnesotans who had never ventured into a Chinese restaurant were introduced to their first taste of chow mein. The Chongs were onto something. More than 40 years later, at the 2002 Minnesota State Fair, attendees dined on stir-fry Szechuan on a stick, compliments of Leeann Chin.[73]

Leeann Chin, probably the best-known Chinese name in Minnesota, also made her cooking debut in the 1970s. Born in Canton, China, in 1933, Leeann and her husband, Tony, moved to the United States in 1956 and settled in Minnesota. Known as a great cook by her friends, her husband, and her five children, she began catering parties and teaching cooking classes in the 1970s and in 1980 published the first of her three cookbooks and opened her first restaurant, Leeann Chin's Chinese Cuisine, in Minneapolis. By 2003 the Chins owned a chain of nearly 60 popular restaurants in the Twin Cities area. Ms. Chin has long participated in community causes. She, along with Weiming Lu, is a member of the Committee of 100, a national nonpartisan organization composed of American citizens of Chinese descent who have achieved positions of leadership in the United States. The mission of the group is to address important issues concerning the Chinese-American community, as well as ones affecting U.S.–China relations.[74]

On the subject of food, it should be noted that the earliest documented serving in the Twin Cities of dim sum, small dishes of food cooked in bamboo or metal steamers and often served from pushcarts, was at the Far East Café in Minneapolis in 1968. Hui Ping James and her husband, Leonard James, owners of the restaurant, also had two retail stores in Minneapolis.[75]

To address the growing diversity among Asian Minnesotans, members of the Asian American Alliance formed the Minnesota Asian American Project (MAAP) in 1977 to promote affirmative action, civil rights, and legal services

Leeann Chin prepared a stir-fried dish as part of a cooking demonstration in 1978.

for the Asian community. MAAP, the first pan-Asian community organization in the state, was initially led by Frances Tsai, who saw the importance of strength in numbers and the need for one visible Asian American group within the Twin Cities. Members included Cambodians, Chinese, Filipino, Japanese, Korean, Laotian, Thai, and Vietnamese, all relatively small in number as communities. The organization was active in challenging racially offensive material in the media and promoting legal defense and education issues. Members of MAAP assisted with the organization of an Asian American Task Force to advise the University of Minnesota's Office of Minority and Student Affairs.[76]

Mandarin Beef

Leeann Chin's use of traditional ingredients and quick cooking methods, exemplified in her classic recipe for Mandarin Beef, has contributed to the success of her restaurants and made her cookbooks best sellers.

1 pound beef, boneless sirloin or
    round steak
1 tablespoon vegetable oil
2 teaspoons cornstarch
1 teaspoon salt
1 teaspoon soy sauce
½ teaspoon sugar
½ teaspoon white pepper
2 green onions (with tops)
1 large green bell pepper
¼ cup vegetable oil
1 teaspoon finely chopped gingerroot
1 teaspoon finely chopped garlic
¾ cup shredded carrot
1 to 2 teaspoons chili paste
1 tablespoon dark soy sauce

Trim fat from beef steak; cut beef lengthwise into 2-inch strips. Cut strips crosswise into 2-inch strips. Cut strips crosswise into 1/8-inch slices. Stack slices and cut lengthwise into thin strips. Toss beef, 1 tablespoon vegetable oil, the cornstarch, salt, 1 teaspoon soy sauce, the sugar, and white pepper in medium bowl. Cover and refrigerate 30 minutes. Cut green onions diagonally into 2-inch pieces. Cut bell pepper into 1/8-inch strips.

Heat wok until very hot. Add 1/4 cup vegetable oil; tilt wok to coat side. Add beef, gingerroot, and garlic; stir-fry 3 minutes or until beef is brown. Add bell pepper, carrot, and chili paste; stir-fry 1 minute. Stir in green onions and 1 tablespoon dark soy sauce; stir fry 30 seconds.
4 servings

MAAP members dispersed in 1984, but a pan-Asian American grass-roots organization called the Minnesota Asian American Coalition (MAAC) was formed to promote the creation of a state council on Asian Pacific affairs. Judy Wong, a war bride baby and University of Minnesota graduate, served as chair. Under her leadership, MAAC lobbied the Minnesota legislature in 1985 to establish the Council on Asian Pacific Minnesotans, an advisory group to the governor and legislators on issues pertaining to Asian Americans. MAAC's foresight was evident when the number of Asian Americans in Minnesota increased from 8,000 to 78,000 between 1980 and 1990. By 1992 there were more than 30 groups under the umbrella of the Council of Asian Pacific Americans.[77]

The University of Minnesota's long-standing relationship with China along with renewed relations between the U.S. and the PRC provided the impetus to establish the China Center in 1979. Located on the university's campus, the Center was founded to manage the school's educational and professional development exchanges with the People's Republic of China, Hong Kong, and Taiwan.

The China Center sponsored seminars and programs on Chinese culture, politics, trade, and development in order to foster a greater understanding of China.[78]

As a result of increased awareness surrounding identity issues, many second- and third-generation individuals began to question what it meant to be Chinese American. Photographer Wing Young Huie, born in Duluth in 1955, noted in a 1979 interview, "There were very few times in my childhood . . . where I thought of myself as being Chinese. . . . I've pretty much lost contact with my heritage. . . . As for my lifestyle, I'm as American as can be." Wing began to explore what it meant to be Chinese in America through writing and photography. His 2002 project entitled "Nine Months in America" represented the accumulation of his travels through 39 states photographing Chinese Americans and delving into their identities, which Huie described as "not easily defined and in perpetual flux."[79]

Achievements and Challenges

The 1980s proved to be an energetic and tumultuous decade for Chinese in Minnesota. After the liberalization of United States immigration law in 1965, Minnesota's Chinese population more than doubled, reaching approximately 4,000 by 1980. A sizable portion of the state's Vietnamese population of 4,500 was actually ethnic Chinese. At this time there were about 150 Chinese restaurants in the Twin Cities, professionals were employed at 3M, Honeywell, and Control Data, and physicians and professors were established at various hospitals and universities.[80]

Minnesota's Chinese-American community in 1981 was composed of a complex variety of subgroups, including young couples and teenagers recently arrived from China, well-established businessmen, students, professionals, and second- and third-generation members. Their lifestyles ranged from that of intellectuals in college towns, who

Chinese New Year's Festivities

One of the earliest references to the Chinese New Year in Minnesota was in the February 14, 1877, issue of the *St. Paul Pioneer Press*. "Monday was the New Year according to the Almanac of the 'Heathen Chinee' and the resident [Minneapolis] Celestials observed it by closing their shop doors, emptying their washtubs, and hanging out their flat irons."

St. Paul merchant Moy Hee used the New Year as a means to introduce people outside of the community to Chinese customs and food. In 1907 he invited more than 100 "white guests" including representatives of the clergy, the bench, the press, the bar, and the legislature. Invitees were treated to an extensive menu and "half-hour ropes of firecrackers." Throughout the 20th century, family and merchant associations as well as student organizations at the University of Minnesota have sponsored New Year celebrations.

Contemporary New Year's festivities continue to serve as a bridge between the Chinese community and greater Minnesota. In addition to special food offerings at Chinese restaurants, a multitude of organizations within the Chinese community sponsor New Year events. In 1991 CAAM led the planning of the largest Chinese New Year's party ever in Minnesota. Jointly sponsored by eight organizations, the party had more than 1,800 attendees and featured a keynote speech by the state governor. In 2003 more than 3,600 Twin Cities-area school children celebrated the arrival of the Year of the Ram with CAAM Chinese Dance Theater at its Fifth Annual Chinese New Year School Show at the College of St. Catherine's O'Shaughnessy Auditorium. The show was designed to entertain and educate the elementary school children about Chinese culture with dance, storytelling, and calligraphy.

Traditional Chinese dance was a feature of New Year's festivities in 2004.

CAAM Chinese Dance Theater's
2004 Chinese New Year School Show

Twelve Animals of the Chinese Zodiac

Fun Field Trip!

Tuesday, January 20, 2004
9:15 am, 11:15 am, 1:00 pm
Tickets: 651-312-0648, Ext. 1

Come celebrate Chinese New Year with us!

· FUN and educational Field Trip!
· Narrated excursion of Chinese culture!
· Performed by Talented Students and adults!
· Educational materials provided for teachers!

were well integrated into local social life, to recent immigrants in the Twin Cities, who sought the support and intimacy of traditional Chinese organizations. The rapid growth and fragmentation of the Chinese settlement in Minnesota after World War II brought many changes in the older organizations and a proliferation of new ones to meet the needs of the subgroups within the community.[81]

The Organization of Chinese Americans continued to seek representation in the 1980s by raising money for candidates running for both state and national offices. Although the Chinese community was still relatively small in number, their efforts did not go unnoticed. Governor Arne Carlson appointed at least ten Chinese Americans to state committees, including the Investment Advisory Committee, the Board of Accountancy, and the Higher Education Facilities Authority.[82]

By 1987 there were at least 27 Asian churches and Buddhist temples in the Twin Cities with denominations of the Asian churches being Catholic, Lutheran, or Evangelical. The influence of previous missionary work resulted in the establishment of a number of Chinese churches in the Twin Cities area. Evolving from a small Bible study group at the University of Minnesota, the Chinese Christian Fellowship (CCF) was officially established and registered with the state in 1958. Joseph C. Wong, a seminary student and member of CCF, was a longtime leader in the church, which grew to be the largest Chinese church in the Twin Cities. By 1980 the congregation was made up of professionals from northern and southern China, the majority of whom had been students in Minnesota during the 1960s. Wong preached in Mandarin, the language of the north, but those attending could use earphones to hear immediate translations into Cantonese and English. Youth groups and adult classes, as well as family fellowships, continued to be divided by language groups into Mandarin, Cantonese, and English.[83]

Chinese American children attending language classes at Westminster Presbyterian Church took part in the Christmas pageant, an annual tradition, in 1950.

In 1989 the Association of North American Chinese Evangelical Free Churches (ANACEFC) developed a ten-year plan to establish five to six Chinese churches in North America by the year 2000 with the Twin Cities being among the sites chosen. Founded in 1990, the Chinese Evangelical Free Church, located in Minneapolis, started its own Sunday worship in Cantonese. Since the church is located near the Twin Cities campus of the University of Minnesota, a Christian fellowship consisting of students from Hong Kong is also associated with the church.[84]

The Evangelical Formosan Church of the Twin Cities began as an informal fellowship of Taiwanese graduate students at the University of Minnesota in 1962. Jih Hsin Yang and his wife founded the church, first meeting in homes and then at a Presbyterian church in Minneapolis. In 1982 the organization obtained its own building on Iglehart Avenue in St. Paul and began offering services in English and Taiwanese.[85]

In the mid-1980s members of the Chinese American

community recognized the need for an organized means of providing social events for elders to maintain a sense of kinship and continuity. They established the Chinese Senior Citizens Society in 1985 and appointed Lu Ung Kang as the first president of the organization. The society continued to sponsor monthly luncheons and an annual New Year's Celebration where several generations of families gathered to welcome the new year. Activities were conducted in three languages: English, Mandarin, and Cantonese. The society also assisted seniors in the areas of health, finance, housing, and transportation.[86]

Chinese Americans in other areas of the state established schools and social organizations to maintain a sense of community. Beginning in 1980, Rochester's Chinese

Jimin Chen shared recent calligraphy work with Jennie Hsiao (left) and Wai Xi Yun at the Chinese Senior Citizens 2003 spring luncheon.

Culture School provided classes in Chinese dance, Tai Chi, Chinese calligraphy, and language. In 2003 Rochester had one of the largest numbers of Chinese living outside of the Twin Cities and was home to the Rochester Chinese Association, the Rochester Asian Organization, the Chinese Federation of Greater Rochester, the Chinese School of Rochester, and the Rochester Chinese Choral Society. The Chinese Student and Scholar Association at Mayo Clinic (MCSSA) was composed of students, scholars, and faculty originally from China. The organization sponsored various events year round. A Chinese Christian fellowship was started by two families in 1972 and evolved into the Rochester Minnesota Chinese Church in 1998. The church was nondenominational and had members from Singapore, Malaysia, the Philippines, China, Taiwan, and Hong Kong.[87]

With the opening of China in 1979, Minnesota business leaders, like their predecessor James J. Hill, were intrigued by the enormous prospect for trade, especially in the fields of agriculture, technology, and medicine. Trade relations with China had reached a low point during the first 25 years of Communist rule, but personal connections previously established by missionaries, teachers, diplomats, and business people served as a springboard for renewed business opportunities. Northwest Airlines also maintained and furthered business exchanges between the PRC and Minnesota in the latter half of the 20th century.[88]

Throughout the 1980s, Governor Rudy Perpich and former Vice President Walter Mondale conducted trade missions to the People's Republic of China. The 3M corporation established an early presence in Shanghai in 1984, and by 1989 some 80 Minnesota companies were conducting business with the PRC. That same year the state established a trade office in Beijing, and Minnesota saw $100,000,000 worth of goods exported to China. After Perpich's initial visit, business or personal trips to

China by state political leaders were conducted almost every year.[89]

Two significant events, nationally and internationally, occurred in the 1980s that demanded further assessment of what it meant to be Chinese American. In June 1982 Michigan resident Vincent Chin was murdered because he was mistaken for being Japanese by Detroit auto workers, who were frustrated by the downturn in the U.S. auto industry. "I think that the Vincent Chin case . . . was a watershed moment for all Asian Americans," said Helen Zia, a longtime national activist and writer. "For the first time, we considered ourselves as a race, a minority race in America that faced discrimination and had to fight for our civil rights. The Vincent Chin case marked the beginning of the emergence of Asian Pacific Americans as a self-defined American racial group." In an effort to inform the public about the implications of this event, the Organization of Chinese Americans sponsored a speaker, and the Asian American Student Center at the University of Minnesota hosted a series of educational forums. Nghi Huynh, a local Asian journalist, wrote several articles for the Asian American press.[90]

On the international level, the PRC government grappled with how to bring resolution to a series of student-led, pro-democracy demonstrations in Beijing's Tiananmen Square in 1989. The government's order to end the demonstrations on April 20 was ignored by the growing number of protestors. On May 4, approximately 100,000 students and workers marched in Beijing demanding democratic reforms.

Reactions to the unfolding events were evident both at the University of Minnesota, which at that time had about 600 Chinese students and visiting scholars, and within the Chinese American community. Students at the university participated in fund raisers, rallies, and vigils in support of students back home and their demonstrations for free speech and democratic reform. They also attempted to keep communication flowing into the country by addressing hundreds of envelopes to China with news of the latest developments.[91]

While protests were taking place on campus, members of the Chinese American community held a rally at the Como Park bandstand in St. Paul. The event was organized by Weiming Lu, national secretary of the Organization of Chinese Americans (OCA); Joseph Lee, national vice president of OCA, and Cheng Jie, vice chairman of the Friendship Association of Chinese Students and Scholars at the University of Minnesota. Organizers called for the overthrow of Deng Xiaoping, circulated a petition, and took up a collection to help student protestors in Beijing. More than 400 people attended the rally.[92]

On June 3 and 4, 1989, the People's Liberation Army crushed the pro-democracy supporters, killing hundreds of protestors, injuring another 10,000, and arresting hundreds of students and workers. More than 500 people

About 400 people rallied at the Como bandstand in St. Paul to show their support for the pro-democracy movement in China leading up to the Tiananmen Square massacre in 1989. Members of the Minnesota chapter of the Organization of Chinese Americans led the protest. From left to right are Weiming Lu, Joseph Lee, and Cheng Jie.

gathered at Westminster Presbyterian Church for a memorial service for those killed in Beijing. A number of groups and individuals initiated efforts to aid the Chinese, especially with medical supplies.[93]

According to the U.S. census in 1990, there were 1.6 million Chinese in the United States and approximately 9,000 Chinese living in Minnesota. Immigrants from Hong Kong, Taiwan, and the PRC included professionals, merchants, political refugees from Tiananmen Square, and immigrants via Cambodia and Vietnam.[94]

In recent years, thousands of Chinese children were adopted in the United States, with Minnesota being home to more than 300 children, mostly girls, from the PRC. All had come since 1992 when the government of the PRC began to allow foreign adoptions. The organization Families with Children from China Midwest was formed to provide support to these families through education and cultural awareness. As of 2003, more than 250 families from Minnesota, Wisconsin, Iowa, North Dakota, and South Dakota belonged to the organization.[95]

Cultural and professional organizations continued to grow in numbers in the 1990s. The Chinese American Academic and Professional Association in Minnesota

Sadie Stone, originally from Fujian province, was adopted in December 1995. Sadie (left) and her sister, Evie, adopted from Vietnam in August 1998, played in the snow in the front yard of their St. Paul home in 2003.

In 2002 Governor Jesse Ventura appointed Regina Chu to the bench of the Fourth Judicial District in Hennepin County. Chu was the first Asian American female to be named to a judgeship in Minnesota. She joined the sole Asian American on the bench in Minnesota, Judge Tony Leung, also from Hennepin County, who was appointed in 1994. Both individuals are of Chinese descent.

(CAAPAM) was founded in 1992 as a nonprofit organization for all Chinese Americans in Minnesota and neighboring states. The organization promoted professional development and networking opportunities among Chinese Americans and served as a conduit to get their voice heard by government agencies, the legislature, and the general public. Chinese American businesses in the new millennium, many of which include offices in China, range from traditional industries to e-business solutions, including high-tech manufacturing, construction, retail and wholesale, import and export, Internet, software, advertisement, professional services, health care, education, hospitality service, publication, and food service.[96]

To assist newly arrived Chinese immigrants and refugees in their transition to American society the Minnesota Chinese Service Center of St. Paul was established in 1999. Services included helping newcomers find a place to live, seek employment, complete paperwork, and fill out immigration forms. The organization also provided classes in citizenship and the English language, particularly for older Chinese. In October 2002 MCSC began an "Adopt-A-Grandparent" program with goal of bringing Chinese elders together with families of adopted children.[97]

The fiftieth anniversary commemorating the end of

World War II prompted discussion and activism within the Twin Cities Chinese American community. In 1995 the community confronted the Minnesota Orchestra over their plans to perform the composition *Requiem Hiroshima*, arguing that Hiroshima should not be mourned without providing the historical context of Japan's aggressive role throughout Asia during the war. Protests culminated in a candlelight vigil by almost 300 people at Peavey Plaza in Minneapolis and with the orchestra rewriting its program notes. In its efforts to continue educating the public about the impact of World War II on China, in 1998 the community organized a citywide forum for Iris Chang, author of the book *Rape of Nanking*, which explores the massacre of more than 300,000 Chinese in a six-week period by Japanese troops in 1937.[98]

Dissatisfied with the lack of any kind of reconciliation addressing World War II, Asian and American composers and musicians—including cellist Yo-Yo Ma—collaborated to write compositions in remembrance of the Asian Holocaust. This six-year initiative resulted in a concert on May 30, 2001, at the Ordway Center for the Performing Arts in St. Paul entitled "Hún Qiáo" [Bridge of Souls]. According to organizer Pearl Lam Bergad, president of the Minnesota Chamber Orchestra, it was one of the first times in recent history that 17 Chinese organizations in Minnesota came together to work toward a common goal.[99]

In 1998 the Minnesota Department of Trade and Economic Development and the China Council for the Promotion of International Trade (CCPIT) signed an agreement to open a CCPIT office in the Minnesota World Trade Center in St. Paul. The CCPIT has only two other offices in the U.S., the others being in New York and Los Angeles. According to a spokesman, "The Chinese are intrigued by Minnesota because of the reasonably high concentration of technology and agriculture. The marriage of the two here is unlike most places in America."[100]

According to the 2000 U.S. census, Chinese Americans were the fourth largest Asian group in Minnesota behind Hmong, Vietnamese, and Asian Indian. At the time of the census, 62% lived in either Hennepin or Ramsey County (9,634 to 11,425.) Outside of the Twin Cities area, there were concentrations in Olmsted County (745 to 854) and Stearns County (261 to 332). Population in the Chinese American community grew between 79% and 116% between 1990 and 2000. The Taiwanese population, which was counted separately from the Chinese, ranged in numbers from 576 to 631. During this decade there was a rise in the number of immigrants from the PRC, many highly educated, coming to the U.S. for graduate and professional education. Some stayed because of economic opportunities, and many entered the high-tech industry.[101]

The Minhua Foundation was created in 1996 to respond to the needs of the large influx of students from the PRC, many of whom were enrolled in graduate school, had young families, and later became permanent residents. Its founder and principal was Wu Jian Xiong, who came to the United States in 1987 to pursue graduate studies at the University of Minnesota and subsequently became an American citizen. Minnesota China Academy, a branch of the Minhua Foundation, was begun in 2000 to respond to the growing need of the American general public to learn Chinese, a phenomenon, according to Mr. Wu, "particularly propelled by the increasing influence of China in the global arena and the growing number of American parents with adopted children from China."[102]

As of 2003, there were 600 students enrolled in the Minhua Chinese School and Minnesota China Academy. Both schools taught the pinyin version of Mandarin, a simplified version of the traditional northern dialect used in the PRC. While the Minhua Chinese School focused on students from immigrant families who spoke Chinese at home, Minnesota China Academy taught students who

Culture and the Arts

CAAM Chinese Dance Troupe, 2002

Chinese Americans have contributed to many facets of culture and arts in Minnesota, especially in the latter part of the 20th century. The Chinese American Association of Minnesota Dance Theater, which began ten years ago, is one of the largest Chinese dance organizations in the Midwest. Under the artistic direction of Shen Pei, the school has seasonal performances and outreach activities. The Minhua Chinese Dance Theater, also officially created in the early 1990s, provides students of all ages with opportunities to perform traditional Chinese dance.

The Minhua Chorus, conducted by Mr. Lei Li, brings original Chinese music to the people of Minnesota. Musicians perform both western classical and traditional Chinese music. Frank Lee and Evelina Chin are members of the Minnesota and St. Paul Chamber Orchestras, respectively, while Zhang Ying, Gao Hong, and Jiasiang Li compose and perform Chinese music and have been the recipients of several awards and grants.

Assistant professor Wang Ping, Macalester College, St. Paul, is the author of several books, including *American Visa*, a collection of short stories, and *The Magic Whip*, her second collection of poetry.

Artist Cheng-khee Chee is a founder of the Lake Superior Watercolor Society and also teaches in the University of Minnesota's Split Rock Arts Program. His distinctive watercolors are exhibited and collected around the world. Yi Kai, who taught painting at a Beijing University, emigrated to Minnesota in 1990. His acrylics and oil paintings combine Chinese motifs and symbols with American themes, words, and symbols in brilliant and joyous colors.

Organizations such as Asian Media Access, Theater Mu, and Asian Renaissance have emerged in recent years within the Asian American community to work collaboratively to create, share, and educate.

Students conversed with their teacher at the Minhua Chinese School in the Twin Cities in 2001.

did not speak Chinese at home. The school also helped immigrants adjust to American culture and promoted cultural and educational exchanges between China and the United States. The mission of Minnesota China Academy was to teach Chinese language, culture, arts, and other related subjects, with its main focus on students who did not have a Chinese language background.

The Chinese American Association of Minnesota continued its Twin Cities Chinese Language School, teaching traditional Mandarin, with an enrollment of nearly 200 students of all ages. Since 1988, the school, in cooperation with St. Paul Community Education, also offered English as a second language class to new Chinese immigrants. *CAAM News and Views* newsletter, published since 1996, was the only bilingual (Chinese and English) newsletter put together by a community volunteer organization.[103]

In 2000 the community continued to look at national Chinese American issues and organized a forum to educate the public about Wen Ho Lee. A U.S. citizen and scientist at Los Almos laboratory, Dr. Lee was accused of stealing U.S. nuclear secrets and placed in solitary confinement for seven months without being charged with a crime. He was released after the federal government dropped 58 of 59 counts with a judge issuing an apology to him. Kaimay Yuen Terry, community activist and chair of the Justice for Wen Ho Lee Committee of Minnesota, raised more than $10,000 to help with Dr. Lee's legal bills of about $1.5 million.[104]

Minnesota continued its goodwill through various organizations that provided medical, social, and cultural exchanges with China. Minnesota Global Volunteers, Children's Heartlink, the Minneapolis Institute of Arts, and the U.S. China Peoples Friendship Association established important relationships with China that not only made available services to people in the People's Republic of China but also furthered Minnesota's understanding of China. Minnesota's efforts were also represented by individuals such as Weiming Lu who served as a planning adviser to Beijing mayor Liu Qi for a range of projects, including development plans for the 2008 Olympic Games to be held in China.[105]

As of 2003, the University of Minnesota had more than 1,200 visiting Chinese scholars and students at the university, the largest population of Chinese on any North American campus. Alumni lived throughout China or chose to stay in the United States although this sometimes meant having to leave spouses and families in China. Since 1982 the China Center has awarded more than 300 travel grants to university faculty to support collaborative research, consulting, and teaching in mainland China, Taiwan, and Hong Kong. Under the leadership of David Pui in the 1990s and Hong Yang after 2000, the China Center continued to move in new directions. One such example was the Mingda Institute for Leadership Training, established in 2001, which provided advanced training for Chinese junior- and senior-level executives from business and public sectors in China.[106]

Minnesota exports to China increased 84% between

2000 and 2002, with China being the state's fourth largest market for exported manufactured goods. Hundreds of Minnesota companies, including 3M, Northwest Airlines, Hormel, Cargill, Honeywell, and law firms such as Dorsey and Whitney, conducted business in China. In 2002 Governor Jesse Ventura led a Minnesota trade mission of more than 100 Minnesota business and community leaders to China, the largest such mission ever organized by any state. The Chinese American Business Association of Minnesota (CABAM) was established in 2002 with the mission to support and promote the interests of Chinese American business owners of Minnesota and to encourage business relationships between Minnesota and China. The organization sponsored seminars and training sessions that addressed challenges, opportunities, and ever-changing economic policies.[107]

Governor Jesse Ventura was the guest speaker at the 2002 Chinese American Business Association of Minnesota conference where he shared observations about his 2002 Minnesota–China trade mission.

While opportunities for the Chinese have greatly improved over the past 50 years, negative attitudes toward those of Chinese descent still prevail. As Iris Chang noted in her book *The Chinese in America*, "Even though many [Chinese] are U.S. citizens whose families have been here for generations, and while others are more recent immigrants who have devoted the best years of their lives to this country with citizenship as their goal, none can truly get past the distinction of race or entirely shake the perception of being seen as foreigners in their own land."[108]

While attending the University of Minnesota, Benjamin Chang was attacked by a mob in a Minneapolis bar shortly after September 11, 2001. They broke beer bottles over his head, resulting in deep lacerations, but no one was ever found guilty for this assault or even questioned. "I was unable to mourn with the country because all I saw was 'USA, USA' on every news channel, and I was shown that I am not white enough to 'pass' as an American. Analysts said that September 11th would impact everyone in a different way, what an understatement! It turned my life around. Growing up in the Midwest my usual experience has been having people admit that they just don't like 'foreigners,' in which category I, or at least my father, fall into. At a certain level, I am lucky there was no masking the normally hollow façade between strangers, when there was a little alcohol running through their veins. There's a reason it's called 'truth serum.' Sometimes I wonder which of the two scenarios is worse. I have scars on my head from this attack, but I can't say they're the deepest I've ever received."[109]

In the fall of 2002 the Minnesota Chapter of the Organization of Chinese Americans sponsored the first annual Chinese Community Expo in St. Paul. The theme of the event was "Get Acquainted, Get Informed, Get Involved." More than 20 organizations, including business, educational, cultural, and political groups, participated in the event and served as reminders of the depth and diversity of the Chinese community in Minnesota. Looking around the room, it was difficult to believe that only 100 years ago these same individuals may have been denied entry into the United States because of their race.[110]

Fortunately, times have changed. Paper sons are a thing of the past. The world is a much smaller place today than it was even 50 years ago with plane travel from China to Minnesota being a mere 19 hours. Individuals immigrating from China are more knowledgeable about the United States, are more educated, and are more fluent in English. Most importantly, Chinese today experience a more welcoming feeling in the United States than they did 100 years ago. They do not expect to return home to China as in the past—"falling leaves return to their roots"—but rather choose to establish roots in the United States.[111]

The history of Chinese Americans in Minnesota has not only been influenced by issues of geography, race, and global politics but has also been shaped by the ebb and flow of Chinese immigration from different parts of the world. Each group of Chinese immigrants has brought its own cultural, political, and economic flavor to Minnesota, weaving the past and present together to create an ever-changing synthesis of "being and becoming."

Personal Account:
My Father, Harry Chin

By Sheila Chin Morris

Leaving a wife and one-month-old daughter, as well as his mother, brother, and sister, behind in China, Harry Chin (Liang Cheung You) ventured to St. Paul in 1940 in hopes of earning money to support his family back home. He found employment at the Port Arthur Café, where he earned $1.00 a day, working 10 to 12 hours a day, six days a week. World War II opened up improved employment opportunities for Chinese, and after two months of schooling, he was hired to be a sheet metal mechanic for Northwest Airlines, where he earned almost $100.00 a week. Unable to communicate with his family in China, at first because of the war and then due to political unrest and the establishment of a Communist government, he chose to start a family in the United States. It was only when the "confession" program was implemented in 1955 that Harry's American family learned of his paper-son identity. A few years later, the daughter and wife he left behind in China once again entered his life. The unforeseen merging of global and family politics eventually found its way to Harry's doorstep. Over the next several years, Harry sought reconciliation with both families, including his biological brothers and sisters. In the 1980s he brought his last remaining family member in China to the United States, fulfilling all family responsibilities. Harry retired at age 75 after working at several Twin Cities Chinese restaurants, including the Nankin, and moved to Waseca, Minnesota.

As knowledge of her family history began to be revealed to her in her early teens, Sheila Chin Morris began an unanticipated journey of self-discovery. "I feel that being the daughter of Harry Chin has given me an incredible depth that not everybody gets to experience. When I was a little girl, there were sometimes when I just hated being Chinese. I always felt pretty naked and pretty raw, but not anymore. . . . I've learned to celebrate my uniqueness." Sheila has been a graphic designer for more than 30 years, specializing in the design of logos, packaging, and book jacket design. She resides in Waseca and works for the Waseca County Historical Society as photo archivist.

Harry Chin in the kitchen of the Nankin restaurant in the 1970s

I remember when I was little and all of our good friends got together for dinners on Sunday afternoons and some holidays. All the daddies were Chinese and all the mommies were white. My mom was of German descent.

I found out later that my mother didn't want my dad to teach us Chinese. In every other way, she embraced Chinese things, but she didn't want to be left out of the conversation between my dad and us kids. She felt left out enough when his friends would come over and speak only Chinese.

Chinese New Year is very nostalgic for me because they don't happen anymore. But, for me, it was immersion in the Chinese side of the family. When we were at home, we would have pot roast on Sundays or roast chicken or something Chinese, barbeque ribs. But, when we went to the On Leong Chinese New Year's dinner, it was a lot of Chinese, a lot of Chinese talking, a lot of, "What did he say, Dad?" There were huge round tables, banquet tables with ten people each. My dad would see friends. He was always so happy when he'd go there because he would see old friends and he could talk Chinese, and they would catch up on news and about what was happening in China and everybody's relatives and if they were okay. They all had relatives in the old country, so if they were helping each other in any way, a new contact or something to help get money or get news or send something or get something from China, then that was an exchange.

The On Leong Association Club was upstairs over a Chinese restaurant. You'd go up the steps and you'd come into the main room, which had a lot of Chinese teakwood furniture and an altar with a Buddha. On New Year's there would be incense burning and oranges and the boiled chicken set before the Buddha. You'd go down a hallway and one side was the big kitchen and there were volunteer cooks every year. Then, on the other side, there were various rooms that you could go into. I think there was some gambling afterwards in one of these rooms. I think that this was also a place for new immigrant Chinese men. If they had absolutely no place to go on their first night, they could always get a bed there before they would find another place for them to stay.

My first memories of visiting my dad at work was when he worked at the Snelling Café on Snelling [Avenue] and Selby [Avenue in St Paul]. We'd always go to the back door of the restaurant, which was a screen door. And, my dad was always dressed in white and he had his long apron on and his cook's hat, which I just loved, the puffy chef's hat. He'd be glad to see us and he'd say, "Well, what's going on, here? Who are these little kids?" It was always a big deal. I always loved it, because the other cooks were always glad to see Harry's kids. So, they would maybe slip us a quarter or tell me how pretty I looked.

If they were proud of their kids, it was known and, of course, they all shared that, too. That's a great, actually, a Chinese characteristic, I think: pride in your children and, then, racking up your grandchildren and showing them off and success. Their children's success meant that they were successful, no matter what they were doing at the time. It goes back further, too. Getting to this country meant that they seized that opportunity and the family is successively successful, so that is a point of real pride.

When he worked at the Snelling, he'd go to work at five-thirty or six in the morning to get all the American food, the roasts and chicken, whatever, going early in the morning. Then, he'd come home at three. He would nap for an hour, go to Kee's Chow Mein at four and work till eight. He did that six days a week, and every other Sunday, he worked an afternoon at Kee's. I remember when I worked with him on Sunday afternoons at Kee's Chow Mein. I started working there when I was about thirteen for a four-hour shift and I'd get five bucks to do that.

I was about thirteen or fourteen when my mother told me that Daddy might get deported. We learned that President [John F.] Kennedy or Congress had said that if you just go through naturalization again, you can stay and you'll be automatically forgiven [for being a paper son] and allowed to stay. I know that was because they found out how many families, American families, were going to be absolutely uprooted and destroyed if they tried to deport all these Chinese fathers. I'm sure most of the Chinese were in business. If they weren't being hired in American business, they were working for Chinese-American businesses and they were entrepreneurs.

I found out that his name is really Liang, so that was a real bolt from left field. Then, my dad had the choice of going with his real name, Liang, or staying with Harry Chin. My dad doesn't like to upset things. I guess it was more important for him to just keep the order that we had had in our lives. The mortgage was in that name. Their marriage certificate was in that name. Our birth certificates were all in that name. Why go through all that change and so he let our name be Chin.

That would be a second regret that I would have—first, he didn't teach me Chinese—second, that he didn't let me have my real Chinese name when he had the opportunity.

One summer when I was fourteen, my mother said that a cousin was going to come to visit from China, that she had just gotten married, that she was Uncle Johnny's daughter—Uncle Johnny was my "paper uncle," the pretend brother, from Milwaukee. Eventually, I was told that she was my sister and not my cousin. She had grown up in Hong Kong with her mother, who had been married to my dad before he left China. It was an arranged marriage.

She was only two months old [when my father left] and that her mother in Hong Kong had matched her with Ben, her husband, because he had American citizenship and he had a business in Philadelphia. He could bring her to the United States so she could see her father and she could live here.

I don't know what went on between my mom and dad over that issue. I never saw or heard fighting or actually, I don't remember seeing any tears either. I remember my mom trying to embrace the situation and make the best of it. I think Susan was polite. I think it was very difficult for her, because her mother was still alive and living in Hong Kong at this time.

My father's first wife's name was Yuet. She eventually came to the United States. They finally did get together after my mom died. They would go visit Chinese friends. I think he introduced her as his number one wife, first wife, which always has priority and automatic reverence. They'd invite my brother and me over on Sunday afternoons and they'd always cook. She claimed us. That was that. She'd just revel in cooking for us. She brought the old ways with her when she came. She brought stuff that he hadn't thought of making for years. There would be these funny little steamed cakes or dumplings and he would show it to me like it was a new artifact. He'd say, "It's Yuet's. I haven't seen it since I was a boy in China. Look at this."

When I first heard about another family, I didn't think it had happened to anybody else but, of course, it's happened hundreds, maybe thousands of times to a lot of these Chinese men who were stranded in America and where they wanted to be, but they couldn't be reunited with their families during the whole Communist era. So many of them started new families, so I know I'm not the only one. But, there aren't too many "paper sons" anymore.

When I was a little girl, there were sometimes when I just hated being Chinese. I didn't want to be different. I just wanted to have blue eyes and light hair. I wanted curly hair. I just wanted to blend. I just wanted to be one of the kids on the block. In some cases I was, but then in some cases, I definitely was not. I grew up with some fear. I grew up with being afraid of people, not knowing whether they were going to love me or if they were going to, when I was a little girl, call me a name. I was thinking about the stereotypes, you know. I'm a Chinese person. Are they going to like me?

Source: Interviews of Harry Chin, Aug. 20, 2002, and Sheila Chin Morris, Oct. 2, 2002, by Sherri Gebert Fuller, Minnesota Historical Society.

For Further Reading

Chang, Iris. *The Chinese in America: A Narrative History.* New York: Viking, 2003.

Choy, Philip P., Lorraine Dong, and Marlon Hom, ed. *Coming Man: 19th Century American Perceptions of the Chinese.* Seattle: University of Washington Press, 1995.

Fuller, Sherri Gebert. "Mirrored Identities: The Moys of St. Paul." *Minnesota History* 57 (Winter, 2000–2001): 162–81.

Holmquist, June D., ed. *They Chose Minnesota: A Survey of the State's Ethnic Groups.* St. Paul: Minnesota Historical Society Press, 1981.

Lee, Erika. *At America's Gate: Chinese Immigration during the Exclusion Era, 1882–1943.* Chapel Hill: University of North Carolina Press, 2003.

Liu, Eric. *The Accidental Asian.* New York: Vintage Books, 1998.

Mason, Sarah R. "Liang May Seen and the Early Chinese Community in Minneapolis." *Minnesota History* 54 (Spring 1995): 223–33.

McClain, Charles J. *In Search of Equality: The Chinese Struggle against Discrimination in Nineteenth Century America.* Berkeley: University of California Press, 1994.

Telemaque, Eleanor Wong. *It's Crazy to Stay Chinese in Minnesota.* Nashville: T. Nelson, 1978.

Tung, May Paomay. *Chinese Americans and Their Immigrant Parents: Conflict, Identity and Values.* New York: Haworth Press, 2000.

Wong, K. Scott, and Sucheng Chan, ed. *Claiming America: Constructing Chinese American Identities during the Exclusion Era.* Philadelphia: Temple University Press, 1998.

Wu, Frank H. *Yellow: Race in America beyond Black and White.* New York: Basic Books, 1981, 2002.

Notes

1. Gail Carlson, *Asians in Minnesota, 2000* (St. Paul: Minnesota Planning, State Demographic Center, March 2002), 3; http://www.demography.state.mn.us/DownloadFiles/pdf/AsiansMN2000.pdf

2. Sarah R. Mason, "The Chinese," in *They Chose Minnesota: A Survey of the State's Ethnic Groups*, ed. June D. Holmquist (St. Paul: Minnesota Historical Society, 1981), 531–32. Sarah Mason was the first individual to compile information about the history of Chinese Americans in Minnesota. She initiated her research in the 1970s and conducted oral history interviews with members of the community; see Asians in Minnesota Oral History Project, 1978–82, Minnesota Historical Society (hereafter MHS).

3. *Daily Minneapolis Tribune*, Jan. 4, 1883, p. 8; *Stillwater Gazette*, Sept. 17, 1879, p. 1.

4. Mason, "The Chinese," 534; interview with Jane Wilson by Sherri Gebert Fuller, Oct. 11, 2002, MHS.

5. Sherri Gebert Fuller, "Mirrored Identities: The Moys of St. Paul," *Minnesota History*, 57 (Winter 2000–2001): 165–66; Erika Lee, *At America's Gates: Chinese Immigration during the Exclusion Era, 1882–1943* (Chapel Hill: University of North Carolina Press, 2003), 12.

6. Mason, "The Chinese," 531.

7. Fuller, "Mirrored Identities," 166. For additional articles on deportations in Minnesota, see *Minneapolis Journal*, Oct. 7, 1904, p. 1, Mar. 6, 1905, p. 6, Nov. 21, 1905, p. 7. For national context, see Lee, *At American's Gates*, and Iris Chang, *The Chinese in America: A Narrative History* (New York: Viking, 2003).

8. Mason, "The Chinese," 536.

9. Fuller, "Mirrored Identities," 166–67; interviews with Harry Chin, Aug. 20, 2002, and Sheila Chin Morris, Oct. 2, 2002, by Sherri Gebert Fuller, MHS.

10. Mason, "The Chinese," 532; Fuller, "Mirrored Identities," 169.

11. *Minneapolis Star Tribune*, June 7, 2002, p. A10; "Shipments of Flour to the Orient, Season 1902–1903," James J. Hill Papers, James J. Hill Library, St. Paul, Minn.

12. Fuller, "Mirrored Identities," 169.

13. Mason, "The Chinese," 535.

14. Mason, "The Chinese," ; Sarah R. Mason, "Liang May Seen and the Early Chinese Community in Minneapolis," *Minnesota History* 54 (Spring 1995): 223–33.

15. Fuller, "Mirrored Identities," 171–72.

16. Wilson interview; Mason, "Liang May Seen," 228; Fuller, "Mirrored Identities," 177.

17. *Minneapolis Tribune*, Mar. 28, 1943, p. 19, Nov. 18, 1884, p. 6, Apr. 29, 1883, p. 8.

18. *Minneapolis Tribune*, Feb. 2, 1912, p. 1.

19. Charles J. McClain, *In Search of Equality: The Chinese Struggle against Discrimination in Nineteenth Century America* (Berkeley: University of California Press, 1994), 279–80.

20. *Minneapolis Journal*, Mar. 24, 1902, p. 7. Union newspapers continued their efforts to "keep this [Minneapolis] a real American city and prevent it from becoming a veritable suburb of Pekin"; see "Chinese Buy McCormick's Famous Café," Oct. 12, 1917, and "Invasion of Asiatics in Minneapolis," July 28, 1916—both *Minneapolis Labor Review*.

21. *Minneapolis National Advocate,* Mar. 8, 1919, p. 4; Chang, *Chinese in America,* 207–8.

22. Mason, "The Chinese," 539, 540.

23. *Minneapolis Journal,* Nov. 8, 1912, p. 1; Fuller, "Mirrored Identities," 174.

24. E-mail from Dr. Ed Wong to Sherri Gebert Fuller, Aug. 1, Aug. 2, 2003, People of Minnesota Project Files (hereafter POMPF), MHS; *Minneapolis Star,* Mar. 11, 1971, p. 6C.

25. *Minneapolis Tribune,* Dec. 18, 1921, p. 1. Minneapolis and St. Paul newspapers provided extensive tong coverage, 1924–25.

26. *St. Paul Pioneer Press,* Oct. 4, 1925, p. 1.

27. On Leong held a national convention in Minneapolis in April 1940. According to the *Minneapolis Tribune,* Apr. 15, 1940, p. 8, one of the "major problems to be discussed is the difficulty of transporting goods to the country because of the undeclared Japanese war on China."

28. Mason, "The Chinese," 537.

29. Mason, "The Chinese," 536.

30. Fuller, "Mirrored Identities," 175; Chang, *Chinese in America,* 197–98.

31. *St. Paul Pioneer Press,* Aug. 5, 1921, p. 1; *Minneapolis Tribune,* Mar. 6, 1906, p. 9; *St. Paul Pioneer Press,* Aug. 9, 1911, p. 10.

32. Fuller, "Mirrored Identities," 175–77. "Before World War I Chinese sent $100 to $200 per year to family back in China." See also notes from interview with Ed Thum by Sarah Mason, June 7, 1979, Minnesota Ethnic History Project Papers, MHS.

33. Mason, "The Chinese," 531, 535–57.

34. *St. Paul Dispatch,* Feb. 1, 1925, p. 26.

35. Mason, "The Chinese," 537–38. Several Minnesota schools have long-standing relationships with China. They include the University of St. Thomas, Macalester College, Concordia University, Concordia College (Moorhead), Carleton College, Bemidji State University, College of St. Benedict/St. John's University, and St. Olaf College; "Minnesota–China Connections," prepared by the Minnesota Trade Office, May 2002, p. 1, POMPF.

36. Mason, "The Chinese," 531, 535–36.

37. Interview with Eddy Wong, Sept 15, 1978, Stearns County Historical Society, St. Cloud; *St. Cloud Daily Times,* Mar. 7, 1972, p. 8.

38. Interview with Marvel and Stanley Chong by Sherri Gebert Fuller, June 10, 1998, POMPF.

39. Interview with Lolita Woo by Sherri Gebert Fuller, June 6, 2002, POMPF.

40. *The Oriental in Minnesota: A Report to Governor Luther W. Youngdahl of Minnesota by The Governor's Interracial Commission,* St. Paul, 1949, p. 21; Chang, *Chinese in America,* 212–13.

41. Chang, *Chinese in America,* 228. The only documentation found relating to Chinese American involvement in World War I in Minnesota was in a photograph of Yep Lun, a laundry owner in Waseca; photograph LU32.257, Waseca County Historical Society. Yep "entered the service June 27, 1918, and served as a member of the 22nd Company, 161st Depot Brigade, Camp Grant, Illinois"; information from Waseca County Historical Society.

42. Mason, "The Chinese," 538.

43. Chin and Morris interviews.

44. Chang, *Chinese in America,* 216.

45. *Duluth News Tribune,* Mar. 11, 1941, p. 6; Chang, *Chinese in America,* 219.

46. Lee Edwards, *The Life and Times of Walter Judd: Missionary for Freedom* (New York: Paragon House, 1990), 92–94.

47. *Oriental in Minnesota,* 22. The Governor's Report contradicts experience of Twin Cities Chinese Americans who recall

mandatory union membership when employed at the Nankin in the early 1940s; telephone conversation with Oy Huie Anderson by Sherri Gebert Fuller, Sept. 5, 2003.

48. Mason, "The Chinese," 538.

49. *Minneapolis Tribune,* Mar. 28, 1943, p. 19; Wilson interview.

50. Wilson interview; Mason, "The Chinese," 538–39.

51. Wilson interview.

52. www.pbs.org/newshour/forum/january 97/hong-kong; Mason, "The Chinese," 538.

53. Mason, "The Chinese," 539.

54. *The Communicator: A Chinese American Club Publication,* May–September 1949, Westminster Presbyterian Church Collection, MHS.

55. Mason, "The Chinese," 539.

56. *Minneapolis-St. Paul Chinese Directory,* 1970 (Wanchai, Hong Kong: Tin Sing Print Press, 1970), copy in MHS; *Minneapolis Star,* Feb. 5, 1951, p. 13.

57. Mason, "The Chinese," 537.

58. Lee, *At America's Gates,* 240–42; www.huaren.org.

59. Mason, "The Chinese," 539.

60. www.tc.umn.edu/~mcsa/new/index.html.

61. *Minneapolis-St. Paul Chinese Directory,* 1.

62. Joe Ling biography, POMPF.

63. Feng Hsiao (Fred Shaw) resume, POMPF; www.shawlundquist.com.

64. Mason, "The Chinese," 539.

65. Mason, "The Chinese," 540; interview with Weiming Lu by Sherri Gebert Fuller, July 3, 2003, typed transcript, POMPF.

66. www.taamn.org.

67. *Minneapolis-St. Paul Chinese Directory,* 1–2.

68. Lu interview.

69. Mason, "The Chinese," 542.

70. Mason, "The Chinese," 540.

71. *MAAP Newsletter,* Mar.–Apr. 1978, Minnesota Asian American Project, Inc., Minneapolis, Sarah R. Mason Papers, MHS.

72. Chang, *Chinese in America,* 308–11.

73. Chong interview; *Minneapolis Star Tribune,* Aug. 18, 2002; www.startribune.com/stories/456/3164526.html.

74. Brenda Kilber, "Leeann Chin: Fields of Joy," *iAm Magazine, Inc.* (Edina, Minn.), July 2001, p. 6–7; *Minneapolis Star Tribune,* Oct. 20, 1986, p. 2M.

75. *Minneapolis Star Tribune,* Oct. 26, 1990, p. 8B.

76. Mason, "The Chinese," 539; MAAP newsletters, 1977–80.

77. *Minneapolis Star Tribune,* Apr. 26, 1992, p. 1F; e-mail from Judith Wong Hohman to Sherri Gebert Fuller, June 30, 2003, POMPF; www.state.mn.us/ebranch/capm.

78. "U of M Officials Plan China Center for Exchanges and Study," University of Minnesota News Service, Feb. 12, 1979, University of Minnesota Archives, Minneapolis. Also see quarterly newsletter *China Center News,* published by the China Center, University of Minnesota.

79. Interview of Wing Young Huie by Sarah R. Mason, Mar. 25, 1979, Asians in Minnesota Oral History Project; www.wingyounghuie.com. "9 Months in America" premieres Spring 2004 at the Minnesota Museum of American Art, St. Paul.

80. Mason, "The Chinese," 531, 538; *Minneapolis Tribune,* Nov. 23, 1980, Picture sec., p. 19.

81. Mason, "The Chinese," 542.

82. *Minneapolis Star Tribune,* Dec. 2, 1991, p. 1B.

83. *Minneapolis Star Tribune,* Apr. 19,

1987, p. 7; www.tcccc.org; Mason, "The Chinese," 540.

84. www.tccefc.ccim.org.

85. *Minneapolis Star Tribune*, Nov. 12, 1997, p. B7; *Merriam Park Post* (St. Paul), Mar. 1990, p. 7.

86. *Chinese Senior Citizens Society Newsletter*, Jan./Feb. 2003, POMPF.

87. *Minneapolis Star and Tribune*, Sept. 12, 1985, p. 4b; http://www.geocities.com/mcssa; http://members.tripod.com/chasteve/local2.html.

88. *Minneapolis Star Tribune*, June 7, 2002, p. A10.

89. *Minneapolis Star Tribune*, June 18, 1989, p. 1D; "Minnesota–China Connections," 1–4.

90. Helen Zia comments from www.asianweek.com/061397/feature.html. See also Helen Zia, *Asian American Dreams: The Emergence of an American People* (New York: Farrar, Straus and Giroux, 2000); Hohman e-mail.

91. *Minneapolis Star Tribune*, May 5, 1989, p. 7B, May 20, 1989, p. 11A. At this time there were also 500 students from Hong Kong and 500 students from Taiwan attending the University of Minnesota, according to the *St. Paul Pioneer Press*, June 6, 1989, p. 6A.

92. *Minneapolis Star Tribune*, May 28, 1989, p. 4B.

93. *Minneapolis Star Tribune*, June 9, 1989, p. 13A, June 12, 1989, p. 11A.

94. www.demography.state.mn.us.

95. *Minneapolis Star Tribune*, June 7, 2002, p. A10; www.fwcc.org.

96. www.caapam.org.

97. www.geocities.com/mn_csc/index.html.

98. *Minneapolis Star Tribune*, Sept. 6, 1995, p. 9A; *Minneapolis Tribune*, Nov. 27, 1995, p. B1.

99. "Hún Qiáo" [Bridge of Souls] program, May 30, 2001, POMPF; conversation with Pearl Lam Bergad by Sherri Gebert Fuller, Jan. 2003, notes in POMPF.

100. "Minnesota–China Connections," 4; *Minneapolis Star Tribune*, May 14, 1998, p. 7B.

101. Carlson, *Asians in Minnesota*, 2000, 3.

102. www.miinhua.org; e-mail from Wu Jian Xiong to Sherri Gebert Fuller, July 11, 2003, POMPF.

103. www.caam.org.

104. *Minneapolis Star Tribune*, Sept. 30, 2000, p. 10, Oct. 2, 2000, p. 4.

105. *Global Business Quarterly*, Apr. 2003, p. 12–14G.

106. *Minnesota Daily*, Nov. 5, 1998, p. 3, Apr. 26, 2000, p. 8.

107. "Minnesota–China Connections," p. 1. This information was distributed as an information guide for those on the mission.

108. Chang, *Chinese in America*, xiii.

109. Interview with Benjamin Chang, National Museum Fellow at the Minnesota Historical Society, by Sherri Gebert Fuller, May 13, 2003, transcript in POMPF. Chang assisted with research for this book. Also see survey conducted by Committee of 100 at www.committee100.org in which one in four respondents expressed "strong negative attitudes towards Chinese Americans."

110. Chinese Community Expo flyer, Sept. 2002, POMPF.

111. John Kuo Weitchen, "Creating a Dialogic Museum: The Chinatown History Museum Experiment," in *Museums and Communities: The Politics of Public Culture*, ed. Ivan Karp, Christine M. Kraemer, and Steven D. Lavine (Washington: Smithsonian Institution Press, 1992), 285.

Notes to Sidebars

Legislation Affecting Chinese Americans: Philip P. Choy, Lorraine Dong, and Marlon K. Hom, *Coming Man: 19th Century American Perceptions of the Chinese* (Seattle: University of Washington Press, 1995), 167–73.

Chinese Store Inventory: Moy Hee Estate Records, Nov. 23, 1921, Ramsey County Probate Court Records, Ramsey County Courthouse, St. Paul, Minn.

Business Partnerships: Fuller, "Mirrored Identities."

Tradition versus Individualism: Seong Moy: Interview with Seong Moy, Jan. 18, 1971, p. 1–10, Archives of American Art, Oral History Program, Smithsonian Institution, Washington, D.C.; James Waltous, *A Century of American Printmaking, 1880–1980* (Madison: University of Wisconsin Press, 1984), 181.

Fort Snelling Military Intelligence Service Language School: Memoirs: Fort Snelling, 1945 (n.p.: privately printed, 1945).

Mandarin Beef: Leeann Chin, *Betty Crocker's New Chinese Cookbook* (New York: Macmillan, 1990), 102.

Chinese New Year's Festivities: Minneapolis Journal, Feb. 15, 1907, p. 7; www.caam.org.

Culture and Arts: Minneapolis Star Tribune, Nov. 1, 2002, p. 8E; summary of Chinese American musicians, information from Pearl Lam Bergad, May 2003, and artists biographies, Feb. 2003—both POMPF.

Index

Page numbers in italic refer to pictures and captions.

Picture Credits

Names of the photographers, when known, are in parentheses.

Acknowledgements

This essay builds on the late author Sarah R. Mason's work in *They Chose Minnesota*. The author would like to thank the following individuals for their input and insight: Sheila Chin Morris, Kaimay Yuen Terry, Linda Wong Hohman, Dennis Wong, Dr. Ed Wong, Weiming Lu, Jane Wilson, Brian Horrigan, Benjamin Chang, Wu Jian Xiong, Oy Huie Anderson, Harry Chin, Howard and Lolita and Barbara Woo, Stanley Chong, Pearl Bergad, Leeann Chin, and the many warm and welcoming members of the Chinese American community. Research assistance was provided by the staff at the China Center at the University of Minnesota, the University of Minnesota Archives–Twin Cities, Pat Maus at the Northeast Minnesota Historical Center, and county historical societies throughout the state. The author is especially grateful to supportive family, friends, and colleagues, to Sally Rubinstein who patiently led a zygote author through the process of writing a book, and to Wayne Fuller whose support and encouragement made this journey possible.

Minnesotans can trace their families and their state's heritage to a multitude of ethnic groups. *The People of Minnesota* series tells each group's story in a compact, handsomely illustrated, and accessible paperback. Readers will learn about the group's accomplishments, ethnic organizations, settlement patterns, and occupations. Each book includes a personal story of one person or family, told through a diary, a letter, or an oral history.

In his introduction to the series, Bill Holm reminds us why these stories are as important as ever: "To be ethnic, somehow, is to be human. Neither can we escape it, nor should we want to. You cannot interest yourself in the lives of your neighbors if you don't take sufficient interest in your own."

This series is based on the critically acclaimed book *They Chose Minnesota: A Survey of the State's Ethnic Groups* (Minnesota Historical Society Press). The volumes in *The People of Minnesota* bring each group's story up to date and add dozens of photographs to inform and enhance the telling.

Books in the series include *Irish in Minnesota, Jews in Minnesota, Norwegians in Minnesota, African Americans in Minnesota,* and *Germans in Minnesota.*

Bill Holm is the grandson of four Icelandic immigrants to Minneota, Minnesota, where he still lives. He is the author of eight books including *Eccentric Island: Travels Real and Imaginary* and *Coming Home Crazy.* When he is not practicing the piano or on the road circuit-riding for literature, he teaches at Southwest State University in Marshall, Minnesota.

About the Author

Sherri Gebert Fuller is a project manager for museum collections at the Minnesota Historical Society. She was co-curator of the MHS exhibit "The Chinese American Experience in Minnesota."

Printed in the USA
CPSIA information can be obtained
at www.ICGtesting.com
JSHW082221140824
68134JS00015B/668